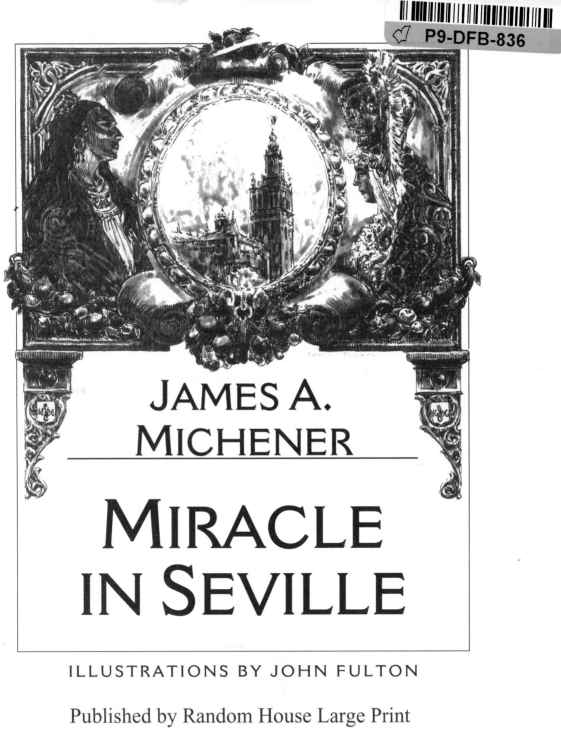

JAMES A. MICHENER

MIRACLE IN SEVILLE

ILLUSTRATIONS BY JOHN FULTON

Published by Random House Large Print
in association with Random House, Inc.

New York 1995

LIBRARY OF CONGRESS CATALOGING-IN-PUBLICATION DATA

Michener, James A. (James Albert)
Miracle in Seville / by James A. Michener :
illustrations by John Fulton.—1st ed.   p. cm.
1. Americans—Travel—Spain—Seville—Fiction.
2. Bulls—Spain—Seville—Breeding—Fiction.
3. Bullfighters—Spain—Seville—Fiction.
4. Seville (Spain)—Fiction. 5. Miracles—Fiction.
6. Large type books.
I. Title.   PS3525.119M56 1995
813′.54—dc20 94-10187

Manufactured in the United States of America
FIRST LARGE PRINT EDITION

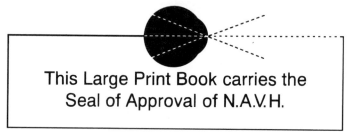

This Large Print Book carries the
Seal of Approval of N.A.V.H.

*This fantasy is dedicated
to that Irish-American leprechaun
Matt Carney
(December 27, 1922–December 24, 1988)*

*A world-class runner
with the bulls at Pamplona*

MIRACLE IN SEVILLE

FOR TWO GOOD REASONS I did not cable New York a true account of what transpired during that spring feria in Seville twenty years ago. First of all, I could not decide if I had seen what I thought I saw. Did it really happen, or was it the product of a mind made overactive by the feverish festivities of Holy Week? Since I kept my writing headquarters in the gracious Alfonso Trece Hotel, I was not far from that famous cigarette factory where Carmen with the rose between her teeth bewitched the Spanish captain sent to guard her. I could distinctly hear her singing at dusk when I passed her factory, so I might also have witnessed other miracles. Even today I cannot be sure of what happened during that vital, spiritual and social three-week fair the people of Seville call their feria.

The second reason for my duplicity was more

simple, but devastatingly effective in keeping me silent. If I *had* reported all of what I had seen to my magazine, my boss would have cabled back: 'Lay off that Spanish wine,' and the conscientious woman who handled my manuscripts, removing the gaucheries in my prose, would have wired: 'Stop your medieval dreaming. Miracles don't happen in the twentieth century.' I could not afford such ridicule.

Now, reflecting calmly two decades later, I suspect that what I experienced was some shadowy glimpse of a truth we men do not like to acknowledge: that women possess an arcane power to influence men, making them see visions and influencing them to perform acts they would not normally commit. I'd struggled through a messy divorce and was already contemplating remarrying, so my thoughts were concentrated on the relationships between women and men. Was I translating my own confusion about women into universal truth regarding their potency? Certainly in Seville I witnessed a battle between two powerful women, and to me they remain as forceful as they were when they involved me in their combat.

I worked in those days for a lively magazine called *World Sport,* which owed its success to a belief that sports-hungry American men would buy a journal that kept them informed about what was happening in the sporting life of countries they'd never seen. One of my more successful stories had been a riveting account of the brave aborigines on Pentecost Island in the New Hebrides who climbed to the top of very tall trees, then leaped headfirst down to earth supported only by vines lashed about their waist and ankles. Make the vines too long, you dashed your brains out. Make them too short and you dangled in midair, an inept fool who would be ridiculed. Make them just right, and you walked away a champion among men.

Since I specialized in bizarre stories, it was my good luck to have seen much of the world's playful nonsense, such as the performance of Argentine gauchos working wonders on the pampas with their bolo ropes, which they could twist perfectly around the rear legs of a galloping horse, or the daring fellows who canoed down the Yukon River during the turbulent spring floods.

My editor had given me the Seville assignment one morning in March: 'Shenstone, we've decided to send you to Spain for a six-pager on a little-known aspect of bullfighting.' When I objected that our magazine had carried numerous takes on that sport as it operated in Peru, Mexico, Portugal and, of course, Spain, the boss rebutted me: 'Sure, Hemingway did that series for *Life* on the summer-long duel between Ordóñez and his brother-in-law Dominguín, and Barnaby Conrad has been effective on the story of Manolete. But what we've never had in America is an honest case study of some typical rancher who raises the bulls that fight the matadors, and we think that the roly-poly in this picture from a Spanish magazine might be just the man we want.'

In the Madrid bullfight magazine he tossed to me I saw the full-moon face of Don Cayetano Mota, owner of the historic Mota Ranch for fighting bulls. He was, the story explained, sixty-eight years old, five feet five, and looked as round as an English toby mug in its three-cornered hat. His thick gray hair was rumpled, just like his suit, and I had the feeling that a man with

JAMES A. MICHENER

a build and a face like that ought to be smiling, but he was frowning as if to say: With me, things are not going well.

I liked Don Cayetano from the moment I saw him scowling at me from the page, an impression that was reinforced when I read additional details about his career: Inherited from his grandfather the distinguished line of Mota fighting bulls whose fame had been well established by the middle of the last century. Exemplars of the breed constantly appeared in the history of bullfighting. One Mota was immortalized by the great Mazzantini, and vice versa. Mota bulls were prominent in those historic fights early in this century in which Juan Belmonte and Joselito contested for supremacy.

The article described how the quality of the line had declined so pitifully during the Civil War in Spain that major matadors had begun to spurn the bulls from this once-famous ranch. The decline continued during World War II to the extent that leading matadors of the postwar period, such as the immortal Manolete and the Mexican Arruza, tried to avoid fighting events in which the Motas were scheduled to appear; even superior artists could accomplish nothing with bulls that were inferior.

When Don Cayetano inherited the ranch in 1953 he had dedicated himself to restoring the Mota name to the glory it had known when Veragua, Concha y Sierra and Mota were the honorable triumvirate of breeders for the plazas of Spain. Unfortunately, Mota seemed to have been waging a campaign that was honorable but doomed—the author of the article wrote that Mota bulls are still more often a disgrace than a triumph. Don Cayetano could take what solace he could from a matchless wall in his ranch north of Seville adorned by the heads of four Mota bulls famous in history. The article was accompanied by a photograph showing the heads handsomely preserved by taxidermists who had polished the deadly horns with wax, and from the photo, which I would want to use in my story, I caught a sense of how majestic and lethal a Mota bull could be. But why were these four special? The text had anticipated my question:

When a bull has performed in some major ring with unparalleled bravery and the time comes for him to be killed, spectators will fill the plaza with a blizzard of waving white handkerchiefs, pleading with the judge to spare the life of this noble animal, which is then taken out of the ring to spend the remainder of his life in pasture. No other surviving ranch can boast of four *indultados.* May the time come again, and soon, Don Cayetano, when you will witness another *indultado* for one of your bulls!

Within a moment of seeing the photo of the four bulls, I knew how my story should be organized: I'll use that word *indultados,* pardoned ones, for the motif. As the Mota bull is sometimes pardoned, so Don Cayetano can be pardoned for the low estate into which his famous ranch has fallen. And Spaniards will rejoice that he's made a comeback, or tried to do so. I like this sentence in the caption: 'When a noble bull is spared, and it happens maybe once in two decades, all

Spaniards seem to rejoice, as if Spain itself has somehow been ennobled.'

I saw the fat little owner, scowling and with shoulders hunched forward as if preparing for battle, as an Everyman who, as the years close in on him, wants to leave behind him some worthy achievement. I would not sentimentalize him, but I would use a portrait of him standing below his four *indultados* to present a warrior fighting to restore his own life. Folding the magazine pages and stowing them in my gear, I asked the secretary in the New York office who handled our travel to get me a flight to Madrid.

I was fortunate that I arrived in Spain at a time when bullfighting, notorious for its violent swings from epochs of greatness to periods of shame, was in a relatively stable condition. If it could boast of no transcendent pairs like Belmonte and Joselito of the 1915–20 period or Manolete and Arruza of the 1940s, it did offer three young men worth seeing whenever they appeared in the ring, for you could be sure they would give an honest account of themselves. They were as honorable in their fields as Joe DiMaggio, Red

Grange, Paavo Nurmi and Don Bradman had been in theirs, and in one significant aspect the matadors surpassed these other greats because when they performed with the bulls they laid their lives on the line. In this century two of the very greatest matadors, Joselito and Manolete, masters of their art in every respect, were gored to death in the ring as thousands watched.

The three noteworthy matadors I encountered were smallish, not much over five feet six, an advantage in bullfighting, where quickness and deftness of movement can mean the difference between life and death. These men were highly skilled artists, built more like ballet dancers than athletes.

Paco Camino was the beau ideal of a matador. Possessed of an elfinlike physique, he was also handsome of face and charismatic in his deportment, exhibiting his skill in the ring with a mesmerizing mix of grace and confidence. On special afternoons he could perform with such perfection that both men and women first gasped at his mastery, then cheered as the graceful Paco circled the ring while the bull he had just killed was dragged away. Nodding to the crowd and flashing a dazzling smile, he would make one tour to the wild applause of the crowd, then another and, at the insistence of the spectators, perhaps a third. On certain memorable occasions, men would leap into the ring at the end of a fight and insist upon carrying him on their shoulders out through the great gates reserved for heroes, *saliendo en hombros.*

El Viti—like many matadors of previous ages, he fought under a *nom de guerre*—was the classicist, a thin fellow slightly taller than his two rivals and whose comportment was marked by a solemnity that never varied. A high priest of the bullring, he was a man of the most uncompromising honor, a figure from ages past who had come into the ring to fight in a mode of classical purity regardless of the quality of the bull he had acquired in the lottery. He presented a remarkable stance when he fought: erect, immobile, face cleansed of any emotion other than dedication to duty, feet fixed in the sand, regardless of whatever ominous moves the bull might make. He seemed at times to be a statue linked with the wild bull in some mysterious way. Men who loved bullfighting revered El Viti for his classic purity and, even more, because he alone still practiced the most difficult feat in the ring, killing *recibiendo* (receiving), which required unbelievable courage and willpower. In the normal final act of killing the bull, other matadors waited till the precise moment the tired bull was about to make a lunge forward, then they also moved forward and leaned in with the sword to gracefully slide safely past the outstretched horns. This in itself is a difficult and dangerous feat. Those who do it poorly land in either the hospital or the morgue, but in killing *recibiendo*—while "receiving" the bull—El Viti did not move his feet at the final moment. Erect and immobile, he allowed the enraged animal to charge directly at him and impale himself on the sword's point. This act is so difficult and so dependent upon the lucky coincidence of timing—the bull moving forward directly onto the sword—that nine times out of ten, no matter how perfectly El Viti has performed his part in the tragic ballet, the attempt fails. The sword either hits bone or misses the mark or is deflected by the bull, and the deadly dance must be repeated. No one jeers at the matador, for he has done his part, standing there impassively as the bull charges at him, and I was to see one fight when El Viti, through no fault of his own, failed six times to kill the bull, with the crowd encouraging him to try yet again. But I was also to see him kill on the first try, with the bull falling dead at his feet and the arena exploding with triumphant shouts as if each spectator had somehow participated in this re-creation of bullfighting's historic days.

The third member of this notable trio was a wild man, as far removed from El Viti as a matador could be. He was El Cordobés, named for his native city in southern Spain, who had discovered early in his life as a street urchin that the bullfight spectators could be brought to their feet by wild exhibitions of daring. Challenging the animal in a dozen tricky ways, his flamboyant histrionics had never before been seen in serious bullfighting. Half circus performer, half matador with superior athletic skills, El Cordobés perfected an exhibitionistic routine that outraged classicists, who wanted to bar him from the plazas, but delighted the crowds, who eagerly crammed into the arenas to see what outrageous thing he would do next. When I first saw him I said: 'This is preposterous! It's not bull-fighting as I know it! And Spaniards who pay good money to see him ought to be ashamed of themselves.' But when I chanced to see him fight in a little town north of Madrid, I saw him give a performance that went far beyond the limitations of classical bullfighting but which retained the ancient thrilling glory of this unique form of entertainment: one solitary man poised against a maddened bull to be slowly and artfully bent to man's will. After a series of awesome maneuvers by both man and bull, El Cordobés had killed with a single thrust, and I had joined the crowd's ecstatic explosion.

So when I reached Spain to write my article on the rancher Don Cayetano Mota and his stumbling bulls, there were these three matadors worthy of attention: Paco Camino, the charismatic; El Viti, the marble statue of rectitude; and El Cordobés, the daring showman.

And there was López.

A lean, long-legged scarecrow of a Gypsy with a scraggly mop of unwashed black hair, Lázaro López

LAZARO LOPEZ

was an unlikely bearer of the hallowed name of matador. As a boy of eight in Triana, the Gypsy quarter of Seville, he had roamed the fields about the city with a gang of boys like himself, making forays at night into the carefully guarded bull ranches. By moonlight he and the others practiced the dangerous art of tormenting young bulls to make them charge. Lázaro never mastered the art of keeping his feet bravely planted while the bulls charged at him, but he had devised a score of rather shameless tricks that tantalized the bulls into charging while enabling Lázaro to give the impression that he was honestly fighting them.

One night when he and his team of young scoundrels had sneaked onto the grounds of the Mota ranch, Lázaro encountered an especially splendid young Mota bull. With the red-and-white checkered tablecloth he had stolen to serve as his cape, the aspiring matador launched a chain of linked passes, one leading beautifully to the next, encouraging the bull to charge the cape again and again. His cheering compatriots spread the news throughout Triana that 'Lázaro López, the scrawny one, he knows how.' As a consequence, some older Gypsies who remembered how their Cagancho, also a tall, shifty man, had become a major fighter in the 1920s and won the grudging admiration of the American writer Hemingway, decided to take young Lázaro under their protection. Since these Gypsies were some of the most venal in Triana, they quickly taught their boy a hundred evil devices.

B ECAUSE of my childhood in New Mexico and my subsequent work in the bullrings of Spain, I speak Spanish easily and also know the lingo of the plazas, tempting me to throw around esoteric words relating to the fight and making me sound more knowledgeable than I am. My editors always restrain me with a sensible rule of their magazine: 'If the Spanish word has found its way into *Webster's Collegiate Dictionary,* use it without italics as an ordinary English word. If it's not there, don't use it. Don't clutter up your manuscript with show-off italics.'

I generally adhere to that rule, for it gives me most

of what I need. Everyone knows toreador, matador and picador, but many may be surprised to learn that 'corrida,' for a full afternoon of six bulls, is also English, as well as the difficult words 'banderilla' (barbed dart) and 'banderillero' (the man who uses it). I was happy to find that the word for the small red cloth used at the end of the fight, 'muleta,' has now been anglicized; I often needed it. I refused to lose *faena,* which designates the matador's entire work in the important last act of the fight, but I could do without *alguacil,* the man on horseback who opens the fight by riding in to ask for the key to the bulls' corrals. There was one forbidden word that is so Spanish and covers such a distasteful part of bullfighting that I would have to use it, rule or no: *bronca.* A marvel of onomatopoeia, it sounds exactly like what it designates: the uproarious riot that can occur at a fight when the audience feels that it has been defrauded and wants to kill the matador. In a *bronca,* with cushions and bottles tossed in the ring, and almost anything else, even human bodies, Spanish bullfighting can be almost as violent as English soccer. *Indultado* is necessary if one is to deal with the emotion of the fight, and I'm also glad that 'aficionado' has become English, for without it I'd miss the spirit of bullfighting. As a bullfight fanatic who goes ape over the spectacle, much like a baseball crazy so intoxicated by his sport that he can even cheer for one of the Chicago teams, I confess that I'm an aficionado.

But I was astonished to find that the one word I needed most had not been anglicized—*toro* for the bull; I used it anyway and without italic. The dictionary did give me a word I used frequently, 'torero,' to indicate all categories of bullfighters. Torero but not toro? Baffling.

THE CLASSIC BULLFIGHT consists of four distinct parts. First, when the bull enters the ring—rushing in if he is brave, sneaking in if not—the matador holds back, allowing his peons to run the animal with their capes held by one corner and dragging on the ground. This allows the matador to study the animal and assess its strengths and weaknesses. But after a few minutes he strides into the arena holding only a large, heavy cape with no appurtenances of any kind. Artfully he plays the bull, attempting arabesques of great beauty. In this first part López could be exciting, unfurling his cape with majesty and drawing the bull into its folds until bull, man and cape formed one solid mass, then suddenly releasing the cape so that the bull thundered past. As an ingenious fellow proud of his mastery of the cape, he devised passes of his own, some of great intricacy, but he became known for the manner in which he performed two traditional passes invented by the great matadors of the 1920s. In the butterfly pass of Marcial Lalanda, López held the ends of the cape behind him with two hands and, body fully exposed to the bull's horns, attracting the bull by fluttering first one wing of the cape then the other. The bull would finally charge at one of the butterfly's exposed wings, then stop in confusion and thrust toward the other. With the matador always edging backward and the bull lunging forward, the two performed a deadly pas de deux. To watch Lázaro López perform the butterfly was to see perfection, and patrons paid large entrance fees to the rings when he fought, hoping to see him perform this dazzling feat. When the bull finally roared past, his horn millimeters from the man, López would lead him past with breathtaking skill, and any true aficionado treasured such an experience.

The second pass, for which López was even more admired, was the Chicuelo, named in honor of the matador who invented it. It had become one of the basic passes that the would-be matador had to master if he aspired to the title. To execute it, the matador held the cape out in front of him, hands far apart to provide maximum target for the bull, then moved forward slowly and artistically, always flicking the end of the cape to attract the bull. When the animal finally charged, the man deftly rotated, snatching the cape away and wrapping it about himself as if it were a flag and he a flagpole.

The trick of this pass was to free oneself from the cape so as to be in position to launch another pass of the same kind before the bull turned to charge again. López was the acknowledged champion of the Chicuelo, and it was his mastery of such classic passes that made the public willing to indulge his sometimes shameful behavior in other portions of the fight. One Spanish critic said of him: 'He's like paregoric, bitter to the taste when he abuses the bull, but good for you because when he does things right you feel wonderful.'

The second part of the fight is dominated by the picadors, massive men dressed in heavy chamois pants, perched on big, ponderous horses and armed with long oaken staves or spears with sharpened steel points. Their job is to position their horses so that the bull will attack and prove his courage while the picador leans forward heavily and drives his lance deep in the bull's shoulder muscles, which are so powerful that unless they are fatigued the matador will have great difficulty at the kill. After the bull staggers away from the horse, the matador has another chance to perform miracles with the cape, and quite often López launched his finest passes at this point.

The third segment of the fight consists of the banderilleros, whose lovely skill usually astounds foreigners seeing their first fight in Spain. These men, usually slim and graceful, have perfected the art of holding two long barbed sticks high over their heads, attracting the bull's attention so that it will charge, and then flinging themselves on a trajectory to intercept the bull. Twisting high on their toes like inspired dancers, and with exquisite timing, they thrust the barbed sticks into the bull's neck to weaken the powerful muscles even more.

Many matadors turned this difficult task over to their assistants, but López, because he was such a skilled trickster and also because his long arms gave him an advantage, took pleasure in doing the job himself, and some of the finest pairs of banderillas placed in Spain in these years were done by him, but he also sometimes had a compulsion to coarsen his act. As a writer from *Sports Illustrated* said: 'Having just planted a pair as elegantly as anyone could hope, the Gypsy apparently felt he had to top even this, so he wrapped the ends of another pair of banderillas in cloth, gripped the bundle firmly in his teeth and, with his long arms fixed closely to his sides, ran at the bull, quartered him, and leaned his long neck over the bull to jab the sticks into the bull. It was the damnedest thing I ever saw, and the most vulgar.'

The fight's fourth segment is somber. The bull, wounded and perplexed, is aware that death looms. The horses are gone. The dancing men with their long sticks torment him no more. The arena is hushed, the matador's subalterns withdraw to safety behind the red protective barrier, and the matador steps alone into the ring with only his muleta, the red cloth so infinitely smaller than the cape used earlier, and a symbolic wooden sword. Now it is truly man against bull, and the bull seems to have the advantage, for the muleta is indeed extremely small and the sword completely harmless.

At this solemn moment the matador is supposed to present a noble figure of tragedy, the hidden sword helping to flare out the cloth to tempt the bull into a final series of passes. Done correctly, these passes can be the high point of the fight, the unbelievably dangerous moment when the matador holds only the small cape in his left hand, the sword pointed downward and behind his back in his right hand to indicate it will play no part in what is about to happen. Watchers hold their breath. The band is quiet. An awesome hush dominates the plaza as the unprotected man edges slowly forward, aware that to reach the tempting muleta the bull's horns must pass only inches from the man's chest. One errant twitch of the cloth and the matador is dead; a masterly twitch and the bull dives for the far end of the cloth in a spectacular pass under the left arm of the matador. It is a moment of death-defying daring unmatched in any other sport or exhibition.

And finally the end of the *faena,* what Hemingway termed 'the moment of truth,' when the matador exchanges the wooden sword for one of steel and faces the bull to deliver the thrust of death. He must stand firm and not allow his fear to show. Again, with the cloth in his left hand, he must lure the bull forward while he grips the sword in his right hand, calculates the exact point of entry and drives the lethal weapon home. The bull staggers, finally collapses, and a subaltern rushes out to give it the coup de grâce with a small dagger thrust into the top of the spinal column.

Paco Camino, the handsome magician with the

dark face and dancing eyes, tried to give his *faena* a touch of grace, determined to give the customers their money's worth. He killed honorably. I liked Paco.

El Viti, feet planted in a chosen spot, awaited the terrible final rush when the bull must impale himself upon the waiting sword. He was the only matador alive willing to risk this ancient style. I honored El Viti.

To El Cordobés the *faena* was apt to be a display of inspired vaudeville, with no sense of impending tragedy. He liked to drop to his knees, his back only inches from the bull's deadly horns, then nod to the wildly cheering crowd. He also liked to do the telephone call, dropping on one knee before the dazed bull to place an elbow on the bull's forehead and his hand against his own ear as if listening to a phone call from the bull. But what sent the crowds into an uproar of disbelief was his trick of kneeling and, as he faced the perplexed bull, taking one of the animal's horns between his teeth. Obviously, if the still-powerful bull made a sudden chop with his head, El Cordobés would be skewered right through the top of his skull. I had seen him perform each of these displays and invariably felt cheated, for at the moment of death he diminished his adversary, a terrible thing for any combatant to do. I did not relish El Cordobés's style, but I was constantly amazed by his courage and his knowledge of bulls. That I had to respect.

And López? No matter how brilliant this angular Gypsy had been in the early parts of his fight, no matter how frenzied and prolonged the cheers he elicited, at the end when his performance should have reached an electrifying climax, he invariably ruined it, humiliating himself, his bull and his public. His behavior with the muleta and sword was dismal, a display of such cowardice as to shame even a callow teenager. If, when he stepped alone into the ring for his *faena,* he saw anything about the bull that displeased him, he flashed signals of dismay to the judge and to the spectators: Can't you see that this bull is plainly in no condition to be fought? or Isn't it clear that this bull is blind in his left eye and will not charge honestly? or Isn't it plain that this bull has been fought before and had a chance to learn tricks? Regardless of the response he received from the judge or from the audience, he then and there declared the bull unfightable, hoping the authorities would return it to the corrals. When they refused, he shrugged his shoulders half a dozen times, turning in a circle so as to address each part of the arena, as if to inform the spectators that he now considered himself free to kill this impossible bull in whatever way he found possible.

Boos greeted this admission that the fight was going to end in a disaster, and when he threw back at the crowd indecent gestures indicating he didn't give a damn what they thought, one of those wonderful *bronca* riots resulted. Any riot in a bullring can be awesome, but a López *bronca* usually had a special force, for even after the customary flinging of cushions and chairs into the ring, the protesters remained unsatisfied. Bottles were thrown at him, and enraged men leaped the barrier and stormed across the sand in an attempt to thrash the Gypsy. Such *broncas* always ended with a dozen policemen rushing into the arena, not to punish the rioters, with whom they agreed, but to form a cordon around López to keep him from getting killed. Some of the most illuminating photographs of Spanish bullfighting are those depicting López being beaten up in the ring by angry spectators or being escorted out by several policemen.

But when López next appeared for an exhibition in any of those towns where he had caused a riot, the same patrons would crowd back into the arena in hopes of seeing him give one of his astonishing flawless performances with the large cape and the banderillas. One critic wrote: 'The chances of seeing this awkward praying mantis performing well are not better than one in eleven, but the chances of getting into heaven are about the same, and on a good afternoon, this man is heavenly.'

It was with this background knowledge that I flew from Madrid to Seville to find that a dumpy little man with black hair reaching down almost to his eyebrows was awaiting me. It was Don Cayetano Mota, as gloomy of countenance as I had expected but eager to show me his ranch, which lay some eighteen miles north of Seville. His first words were 'I'm taking you to see the Mota bulls. I want you to live with them, to learn why they're such wonderful animals.'

As soon as we passed through the ranch gates, a pair of pillars dating from past times, I saw that it was one of those Spanish ranches that delight the eye: low, rambling farm buildings erected in the eighteenth century surrounding a fine house built in the late 1880s. The private bullring, a small affair built of beautiful stone quarried nearby, dated back to the 1840s, but the American-style silos for storing feed for the animals were more modern.

Despite the impressive structures, the glory of the establishment lay not in the cluster of buildings but in the broad and rolling fields in which the bulls were bred and grown almost to maturity. The Spaniards had learned when they acquired these bulls from Roman sources in the time of Christ that if they allowed them to grow to full maturity they would be so powerful that no one man could handle them throughout all four segments of the fight. A full-grown bull of massive size and power could topple any horse that opposed it, and when it came time to place the sticks, no man could reach over the enormous, fully matured black hump of fat and muscle protecting the neck. In their sixth year the massive bulls could annihilate a man, so they were fought by the aspiring matadors during their third year. Full matadors fought bulls in their fourth year and, if the breeder felt he might get away with it, occasionally in their fifth.

'These are the Mota ranges,' Don Cayetano told me as we stood on a slight rise surveying them, 'and out there are my two-year-olds.'

'No fences?'

He laughed: 'No one would have enough money to fence a bull ranch.'

I spent four rewarding days at his ranch, talking with him about the history of his bulls. He spoke no English. As a proud Spanish landowner he believed that the world began and ended in Spain and that to learn any foreign language would be a waste of time, for why would he wish to converse with Frenchmen, Germans or Americans? His world was Spain, and even within that big country his focus was exclusively centered on his ranch and the bullrings in which his animals performed. Since I was fluent in Spanish, we conversed easily as he showed me mementos from past centuries: the colorful posters hailing his bulls, the stuffed heads of bulls who had given noble performances, their ears always missing to indicate they had been granted to the matadors who had killed them in high style, and the wall to which my eyes returned repeatedly, the one displaying the four Mota bulls of legendary bravery who had been given the *indultado*. I was gaining a strong sense of the glory that had once accrued to the name Mota.

The present condition of the ranch was revealed that first Sunday when six of its best bulls were fought in the notorious waterfront town of Puerto de Santa María halfway between the famous city that gave sherry wine its name, Jérez de la Frontera, and the seaport of Cádiz, which bold Sir Francis Drake had invaded in 1587 to sink an entire fleet of Spanish ships. 'Singeing the king of Spain's beard,' the feat had been called, for it disrupted Spain's plans to invade England and gave Queen Elizabeth another full year in which to

PUERTO DE SANTA MARIA

plan for her defense against the great Armada when it did arrive in 1588.

Puerto de Santa María was highly regarded in bullfight circles because its corridas offered the biggest bulls rather than the scrawny little things, with the tips of their horns shaved away, so often seen in the smaller towns. The saying was: 'He who has never seen the bulls at Santa María has never seen bulls,' and since I fell into that category I was eager to remedy the oversight.

As Don Cayetano and I drove down from his ranch to Santa María he explained the peculiar circumstances surrounding this fight: 'Traditionally the season begins on the Sunday after Easter in the third week of the great Feria de Sevilla. But since Easter is so very late this year, the impresario at Santa María decided to slip this fight in ahead of the feria. It should be a good one because we'll have three of the top matadors, Paco Camino, El Viti—and López.' I noticed that when he mentioned the last name he dropped his voice, and I supposed it was because he held López in contempt. But what he said next revealed his fear of the Gypsy: 'I'm never at ease when López fights my bulls. Suppose I send a great one to Santa María? And in the lottery, López gets him? He can destroy the best bull ever bred. Fight him disgracefully, so what happens to me? Instead of touring the arena because of my great bull, I have to crouch in a corner as the aficionados riot. Damn the Gypsy!'

Later he confided: 'This year I've sent the best bulls we have to Santa María, because this fight is vital for our ranch. First of the season and all the bullfight critics on hand to see how our bulls do.' When I said nothing, he corrected himself: 'Not the very best bulls we have. We're saving them for the final fight in the Feria de Sevilla. For that gala they must be good.'

It was a grand day in Puerto de Santa María. The hot sun was cooled by a soft breeze from the sea, and a large number of men and women who loved bullfighting roamed the streets. The plaza outside the arena was crowded with booths selling black-cloth bulls with enormous polyurethane horns, banderillas with sharp points, baby-sized bullfight capes and gaudy posters of the town and its prized bullring. This was a true Spanish festival.

According to custom, the owner of the ranch that supplied the bulls for a fight was given private quarters in an almost completely enclosed box under the stands, from which, through a narrow slit, he could follow the performance of his bulls without being disturbed by the crowd. Sitting in the box with Don Cayetano and fixing my eyes on the festive gate through which the three matadors and their teams would soon appear, I told my host: 'Considerate of the plaza to give you a box like this,' but he replied: 'They do it so that the crowd can't throw things at the owner if his bulls are bad.'

Now the clock stood at one minute to five in the afternoon, that magical moment *'a las cinco de la tarde'* which the poet García Lorca used to such mesmerizing effect in his lament for a good bullfighter. As the big hand of the clock inched ahead, we all stared upward at a gaudily ornamented box high above the other seats where sat the civil official known as el presidente, who was responsible for the orderly progress of the fight. His decisions were conveyed to the toreros below by a signal flashed with a white silk handkerchief, and his orders had to be obeyed by everyone in the ring.

At five sharp he gave a signal to the seven-piece band perched opposite him in its own crowded box and a lively taurine paso doble echoed across the arena, whereupon, from a small red gate appeared an official dressed in medieval costume and riding a white horse. He went to seek permission from el presidente to start the fight and, permission received, galloped back to the main gate to inform the toreros that the fight could begin.

A bugle sounded, the gate swung open nearly in

our faces because our box was so close to it, and out marched the thirty-six toreros in a parade unmatched in any other sport. Almost shoulder to shoulder, as if they were a team of brothers, came the three matadors. In obedience to an ancient tradition, the senior in point of service was on the left, the next senior on the right, and in the middle the matador who had most recently attained the title. On this day it was Paco Camino left, El Viti right, with López in the middle. Strung out behind each matador came his three banderilleros and his burly picadors. Bringing up the rear were the peons driving the mules and bearing shovels. Their job was to tidy up the sand after each of the six fights.

I admired the handsome appearance of Paco Camino and El Viti, while I was amused by the ungainly figure in the middle—the scarecrow López looked completely out of place, his awkward stride a half-beat off the count. And as if that were not enough, behind him came not a handsome slender banderillero but a shortish fellow with a suggestion of a hump on his back. He looked strange and I asked Don Cayetano: 'How can that one place the banderillas?' He replied only: 'You'll see.' Following him came another grotesque creature, half horse, half man. He was the picador of the López troupe, a huge fellow who must have weighed nearly three hundred pounds, dwarfing his horse. Indeed, the man in his leather suit seemed so heavy that even though the horse was sturdy the monstrous man caused a pronounced dip in the middle of the animal's back.

López with his two misshapen toreros looked so ludicrous in contrast to their handsome colleagues that I asked Don Cayetano: 'Why are they allowed?' and he said: 'López has planned it that way. They're so bad that when he's good, he seems very good indeed. But of course he's never good when he fights my bulls. You can expect a disaster.'

As he uttered this gloomy prediction he crossed himself and offered a brief prayer: 'Virgin Mary, let my bulls be good on this important day.' I realized how important this particular fight in Santa María was, for if his bulls were as bad as they had been recently, the press would announce: 'Once more the bulls of Don

Cayetano gave a miserable account of themselves . . . little better than overage oxen picked off the streets.'

Now the trumpet sounded, shrill and brassy, and the small red gate leading from the bull pens swung open to admit what looked to me to be a handsome young bull in his prime, and the applauding crowd must have judged him the same way. But then I saw Don Cayetano cringe and suck in his breath, as if he were whistling in reverse, and when I looked back into the ring I saw the fine-looking bull behaving in a cowardly way. He would not charge the capes of Paco Camino's men. He ran in terror from the horses, and he showed no disposition whatever to follow the matador's big red cape. He was a disaster, and within five minutes from the start of the afternoon, the crowd was booing the bull and whistling derisively.

That was the start of as painful an afternoon as I would ever know, because I had to sit there beside Don Cayetano in the darkened breeder's box and share intimately with him the humiliations of that long day. With the first bull Paco Camino could do nothing. The second bull was a fraud which allowed El Viti to stand motionless before him and await a charge that never came. When López faced the third bull, catastrophe invaded the plaza, for the bull was so bad that the scarecrow could not even try one of his poetic passes. The animal was so cowardly that when the time for killing came the audience demanded it be returned to the corrals while a substitute from another ranch with a better reputation was brought in. But even though the substitute was a decent bull, López could do nothing with it either.

At the halfway mark, when mules hauling rags circled the arena to smooth the sand, I could not escape an unworthy thought: This day must be agony for Don Cayetano, with all his dreams collapsing, but it's good for my purposes because it will allow my readers to feel in their guts the distress my little hero is experiencing. As I thought these ungenerous words I heard Don Cayetano praying again: 'Holy Virgin! One boon only. Let the last three be acceptable bulls, let me know again one afternoon of glory.' I should have allowed him to pray undisturbed, but I had to ask: 'What did you mean by that last bit?' and he was so eager to re-gale me with bullfighting lore that he showed no irrita-tion at my rude interruption.

'I have known afternoons of glory, but not many recently. And Mota bulls have been sent from the ring alive with bands playing—*indultados,* because they were so brave.' He sighed: *'Indultados,* the highest honor, happened three times with my grandfather, but it's happened to me only once and that was long ago.' Suspecting that he wished to speak about that glorious day I asked: 'Where did it happen?' and he said: 'Bil-bao, that city up north where they fight the biggest bulls in Spain . . . It was a memorable bull, Granero by name, because as a calf he used to break into the feed bins. That afternoon the crowd demanded that his life be spared—there was enormous shouting at the president, who finally waved his white handkerchief. When Granero rushed out of the ring the entire crowd shouted *"Ganadero!* the breeder," and I was invited to make two circles of the ring to honor my great bull.'

Turning suddenly to face me he said solemnly: 'I swear to you that I shall see an afternoon like that again. My bull leaving the ring in glory, I walking behind to cheer his going.' He spoke with such fervor, such determination to continue working with his ranch until its reputation was restored, that I reached across to embrace him: 'It will happen, Don Cayetano. I feel it.'

It did not happen in Puerto de Santa María. The rough-and-tumble patrons in that town were in no mood on the opening day of their bullfight season to tolerate the inadequate bulls that the Mota ranch had sent them; when the fourth bull, belonging to Paco, refused to follow the cape or give any show of bravery whatever, cushions began littering the ring in censure not of the matador but of the bull—of all the bulls of this afternoon, the disgraceful bulls of Don Cayetano.

When El Viti strove desperately to construct a respectable fight with the fifth bull but failed because the bull would not cooperate, objects began to rain down on our box with such force that I whispered to Don Cayetano: 'I'm glad the roof is solid.' He merely groaned, and then I heard him praying again: 'Virgin Mary, one boon, please! Let this last bull do well. Let him save the day for us.' I realized that he was making me part defender of his ranch, and I found myself praying, too: 'Let's have one decent bull, Mary. Give it to the old fellow. He really needs it.' It must have been my prayer that did the trick, for the sixth bull, the last of the afternoon, roared into the ring prepared to confront whatever enemies lurked there. With powerful snorts he attacked the capes the López peons trailed before him with one hand. The lanky matador, sensing that he had a good bull, ran out to assume command, and the bull stuck his nose in the cape and kept it there, permitting the Gypsy an opportunity to unfurl a series of linked passes that brought wild cheers.

The bull wanted to fight and charged the horses several times with great vigor. When he passed the bull on to the banderilleros, López revealed himself as the master manipulator. Just as his humpbacked peon was about to start his run on the bull, López grabbed the sticks from his hands and dismissed him so that he could show off his own superior form. I must admit he did place the sticks well, three pairs of them, but his contemptuous treatment of his peon repelled me.

The afternoon had been saved, for the aficionados of Puerto de Santa María acknowledged that they had seen a master artist engage a good bull, and I was heartened by the cheers that now rained down instead of seat cushions and jeers. The change in mood had been dramatic, but it did not delude Don Cayetano, for he gripped my arm: 'No cheering, please. With López you never know till the bull is safely dead and out of the ring.'

He was prophetic, because when the time came for the Gypsy to step forth with his muleta and sword, all courage departed. He had proved that the sixth Mota bull was an exceptional beast but was now terrified of it, and in a most shameful display he tried to convince the judge and the crowd that the bull was defective and could not properly be fought with the muleta. I heard him addressing the people near our box: 'Too dangerous! This one does not follow the cloth. His left eye, you can see it's defective.'

Not even stern orders from the judge or condemnations from the crowd gave López the courage to face this honest bull, and as the Gypsy made one futile pass after another I cried to Don Cayetano: 'If this bull had fallen to one of the other matadors, he'd have immortalized it.' But the Don did not hear my consoling remarks, for a roar of disapproval accompanied an avalanche of pillows. The aficionados of Santa María, some of the most knowledgeable in Spain, were being defrauded, and they were vocal in their anger:

'*Cobarde!* Coward!'

'*Sinvergüenza!* Shameless one without virtue!'

'*Asesino!* Assassin!'

López ignored the derisive shouts and made no effort to kill the bull honestly, running instead in a wide circle and trying to stab it to death without ever placing himself in danger. A full-scale *bronca* ensued, with cushions littering the arena and chairs being thrown at López, who, with the sweat of fear staining his suit, tried vainly to hit a vital nerve in the bull's neck while running away from the animal. It was shameful, the worst *faena* I had ever witnessed, and I grieved with Don Cayetano as I saw this splendid toro, who might have saved the afternoon had he been fought properly, so abused because a cowardly matador did not know what to do with it.

'This is awful,' I told Don Cayetano, and he said bitterly: 'With López, a born coward, what else can you expect?' When the bull was finally killed by a glancing, running stab, the arena filled with angry men wanting to beat López senseless, and the police streamed in to form a protective cordon around the matador. I again had two conflicting thoughts: What a tragedy for Don Cayetano. What a marvelous scene for my article. I hope I can buy some good photographs of the riot.

As the long day ended, the pathetic man at my side angrily muttered through his teeth: 'That López! Someone should murder that coward,' and I was inclined to agree with him, for if a matador does not have a true sense of honor, the bullfight falls apart and its very essence is destroyed. Paco Camino would have used his muleta to work a miracle of passion and beauty with that sixth bull. El Viti would have stood like a noble statue, feet firm, as he drew the bull toward him in a culminating moment that would have caused the crowd to gasp in wonder. López not only failed to accomplish such a feat, but in his cowardice he denigrated a noble animal. I understood why Don Cayetano might contemplate killing him, for López was ruining the Don's chances of revitalizing the Mota bloodline.

To celebrate properly the famous spring feria in Seville requires three full weeks. The first begins on Palm Sunday and runs with great religious passion till Easter Sunday, the day when Christ rose from the dead and entered heaven. The second week is given over to quiet reflection, but the third is marked by an explosion of magnificent activity. There is a bullfight every afternoon for eight days, Sunday through Sunday. Parades in the park. The performance of bands and orchestras. Theaters giving plays. And above all, hundreds of tents are pitched in a bosky wood for the duration, and there the people of Seville entertain their friends—and any strangers to whom they have taken a liking.

These three weeks present the finest spectacle in Europe. There may be certain extravagant celebrations in Asia that equal it, and I have friends who say that nothing can surpass Carnival in Rio, but I'll take Seville in the three weeks after Palm Sunday. Then the historic streets and narrow alleyways of the city are filled with barefoot penitents laboriously carrying crosses eight feet high, such as the one Jesus bore on his way to Golgotha. Men of substance in the city—bankers, generals, elected officials—often appear in the processions in penitent's rags, bearing their crosses to demonstrate to the public that they share the tortures that our Lord suffered.

Bands also parade along the same streets and alleyways, but the climax of each day comes at dusk, when the huge floats that have made the city famous for its piety emerge from Seville's many churches. These are monstrous affairs, sixteen or eighteen feet long, but no wider than six or seven feet so that they can navigate the narrowest corners. Each provides a platform for some huge religious statue, such as an oversize replica of the Virgin or a meticulously carved

diorama depicting a scene showing Jesus at some point on the Via Dolorosa or at the Crucifixion. On some of the big floats actors in fine costumes represent Roman soldiers or Pontius Pilate rendering judgment.

The massive floats are unique. Each of some sixty churches sponsors a float, but only a dozen or so are paraded on any night of Holy Week. One of the more spectacular displays comes from a small church in the Gypsy quarter of Triana across the Guadalquivir River from Seville, and although the float is properly known as the Virgin of Triana, in the street it is affectionately called La Virgen de los Toreros, the Virgin of the Bullfighters, for it displays in carvings unmatched by the other floats a beautiful Virgin bestowing benediction on a dying matador who has been killed in the Maestranza, Seville's classic arena. Three members of the matador's troupe—peon, banderillero, picador— attend the apotheosis, the last astride a stuffed brown horse in better condition than those seen in the ring. When this float passes through the streets on its appointed night, Maundy Thursday, the people of Seville bow reverently, for this is a death scene that frequently occurred in that city prior to the discovery of penicillin, which now keeps many matadors alive even when a bull's horn with a jagged tip invades the belly or the intestines.

The platforms on which the figures, carved or real, stand are about four feet from the ground, and the bottom of the float is covered by a gray cotton cloth so that spectators cannot see the two dozen or so sweating workmen who carry the float on their bent-over shoulders. It is brutal work, but the men of Seville seek it. Like the leading citizens who drag their crosses through the city, these workmen want to offer penance to the memory of Jesus who died for them. This work in the dark is so strenuous that each float, as it progresses slowly and funereally through the city on its two- or three-hour circuit, halts at short intervals to rest on wooden legs hidden at the four corners. Then the sweaty men, often bare to the waist, are free to look out from under the cloth hiding them and implore bystanders to offer them a drink.

When the Virgin of the Toreros passes on its Thursday procession prior to the awful solemnity of

Good Friday, there are many stops and much imbibing and even a certain amount of frivolity, for the toiling men know that on Friday, the day Jesus died, there will be neither drinks nor celebration.

As Holy Week approached this year, after the debacle at Puerto de Santa María, I asked Don Cayetano what he would be doing and whether he would allow me to accompany him in order to flesh out my story. Having seen how serious I was about my work and how eager I was to depict him as he was—never a hero, never a braggart, always a somewhat downtrodden little man striving to protect the honor of his family name and the reputation of his ranch—he pleased me by saying: 'For these three weeks, where I go you go.'

On Palm Sunday he rose early at his ranch and inspected the six bulls he would be sending to Málaga for the big fight there on the Sunday after Easter, assuring me that at least three of them were as good as that sixth one at Santa María. Then he said: 'Now to the carpenter's shop,' and he showed me the seven-foot cross made of some light wood from Brazil that he proposed to lug through the streets as proof of his willingness to undergo the same kind of torment Christ had suffered on the Via Dolorosa; and as I would discover later, he was also seeking special consideration from the Mother of Jesus. When I tried to heft the cross I was appalled by its weight, but he explained: 'I don't carry it. I drag it,' and he showed me a polished metal plate at the foot that would ease the cross's passage over the cobbled streets.

'It can be done,' he said, 'and I must do it.'

Before loading his cross on the small truck that would deliver it to the cathedral doors in Seville, he went into the chapel his family had maintained next to the small bullring for the past century and a half, and there I overheard him utter a fervent prayer: 'Mother of God, allow me just once to guide my bulls. Help me to help them perform respectably. Help me! Help me!'

On the way into Seville I asked: 'What did the prayer mean?'

'You were not supposed to hear,' but with obvious reluctance he shared his daydreaming: 'Since boyhood I've imagined this perfect fight, especially in these years when the ranch seems to be slipping backward. A Sunday in Seville—it would have to be Seville. Matador Diego Puerta for honor. Curro Romero for local patriotism. El Cordobés for display, and six brave Mota bulls.' He paused, then apologized: 'Of course, all ranchers have that dream—maybe with other matadors, but always with their bulls.' He laughed nervously, his round face lighting up with the flow of his dream: 'But mine's different, because in my dream I *am* the bull.'

This amazing statement demanded an explanation, and he elaborated almost eagerly, as if having gone this far he had to go all the way: 'When the trumpet sounds for my bull to enter the ring, I leave this box, fly across the sand, and run with him—inside—bringing with me all I know about how a bull should behave. I become part of his brain to give him wisdom, his heart to give him courage. I am what you might call a living part of my bull's mechanism.'

'That would make a powerful bull, but it would require a miracle.'

Seeming to accept the idea of a miracle, his voice

deepened. His pronouns changed and he no longer discussed the bull as a separate entity; he became the bull: 'I come roaring into the arena, hooves flying and kicking up sand. I snort. I look in all directions and when I see a cape I drive directly at it, and if the matador is skilled I follow the cape and not him, and as soon as I roar past, as close to him as possible, I stop short, turn quickly and ready myself for another perfect pass and then another, until the entire arena is screaming with delight at the way I and the cape and the brave man form sculptures.

'Then, the skilled matador dismisses me with a masterly twist of his cape, which leaves me facing one of the picadors. I snort and paw the ground, trying to look fierce, and making sure I am not too far from the horse—lest my charge have such momentum that I destroy him—I lower my head and drive directly at that pointed spear. That spear hurts, dreadfully, but I am a brave bull, so after the picador drives me off, I slide right into the waiting cape and the matador and I do some Chicuelo passes and a series of four butterflies, first to one side of the matador standing unprotected before me, then to the other, a beautiful dancing until the crowd roars again.'

He was so intimately involved in being one of his bulls that he seemed to lose pounds and become a lithe creature, a young bull in full command of his powers. 'Now I give the banderilleros a chance to display their skills, but if only the peons place the sticks I perform nothing special. If the matador himself wants to try, I move in trajectories so perfect that the crowd sees wondrous sights.' He paused as if savoring the beauty of that moment, then continued, once again identifying totally with his bull.

'Then comes the climax I've been waiting for. All my heroics lead to this, when the matador returns to the ring to face me with only that small muleta and the sword. Because I want the fight to end on a note of perfection, I follow the dancing muleta wherever it takes me, and in the closing moments when the matador stands unprotected with the muleta almost behind him so that I must pass his body before I reach the cloth, I charge straight and true—once—twice—three times till the crowd reaches the point of ecstasy.'

I paid him the courtesy of hearing him through, but when he did not explain how, as the bull, he escaped death in the final moments when the matador leveled his sword at the fatal spot in the bull's neck, I asked him. 'Simple,' he said. 'Seconds before that fatal moment arrives my spirit quits the bull's body and returns to its place in my body—in the rancher's box under the stands. From there I watch the triumph of my bull as the mules drag his dead body three times around the arena and out the gates to immortality. That's how Mota bulls conducted themselves in the old days and that's the way I'd act if I could be one of my bulls today.'

Looking sideways at Don Cayetano as we drove into the outskirts of Seville, I thought: This man is near crazy—he has a fixation, an obsession. He sits here beside me, a seemingly ordinary man, but he's really inside the heart and mind of one of his bulls. If he were given to violence he could be quite dangerous. In fact, if he was near Lázaro López when the Gypsy mal-treated a Mota bull I'm sure Don Cayetano would kill López. He said as much. He certainly seems crazy, but I won't be able to say so in my article.

I had already learned of Don Cayetano's tendency toward mysticism in a most revealing interview when I visited a priest in the village near the ranch. A young man with an obvious passion for rectitude in his little community, he spoke with a mix of enthusiasm and reverence: 'It wasn't easy for me, coming as a young seminary student to a church where the leading citizen was an elderly man as distinguished as Don Cayetano, and at first I was in awe of him, while he was suspicious of me. But when his daughter, Inés, was thrown from her horse and lived for several weeks hovering between life and death, I could not ignore my task of praying for her and giving what comfort I could to Don Cayetano and his wife, María Concepción. They may have thought I was too young, but since I was with them daily, and since I had known their daughter as a delightful young woman who had wanted me to officiate at her wedding, I stayed close to the ranch. When Inés died, I said the prayers at her grave and consoled Don Cayetano and Doña María Concepción as best I could.'

'Were they shattered?'

'Dreadfully. The light of the world went out for them, and I believe this accounted for the mysterious decline of Doña María. To this day it remains a mystery. My own belief is that in the heart of her being, where decisions are made, she gave up. You've heard the words "She wasted away"? She decided to die and she did.'

'And Don Cayetano?'

'It was then we became intimate friends. I had prayed with him daily and tended Doña María spiritually, advising them both to place their trust in the Virgin Mary. They did, and in Doña María's final days a kind of benign grace settled upon them, as if they accepted the dual tragedy that had struck them. One day Don Cayetano told me: "Father Eduardo, your prayers have brought us into the arms of the Virgin Mary," and he and Doña María became convinced that the Virgin herself had come into the sick chamber to guard over them. Doña María died in extraordinary grace and ease of mind. Don Cayetano assured me that in the death chamber he had found a friend for life, and at first I thought he meant me. Not at all: "In the moment before my wife died, I felt a presence come into our room; she felt it too. And when we looked, there stood the Virgin, clothed in blue and radiance. In a voice as clear as a bell she told us that since we had prayed with dedication and belief for her assistance, she had come to take Doña María home." '

Father Eduardo added: 'In the days after the funeral, daughter and mother lying side by side in the Mota crypt, Don Cayetano gave me a huge gift for the rebuilding of our little church and paid a substantial sum for a fine marble statue. The Virgin of Mota, the villagers call her, and if you look over there you can see her bestowing her blessing upon us.'

At this point the priest hesitated in a manner that made me suspect he had more to tell me, so I said as casually as I could: 'You look as if you knew something more that might help my story,' and he laughed, all tension gone: 'That's why you're a good reporter—you see important things. Yes, there was something mysterious about the vision Don Cayetano had of the Virgin. In rural areas priests often meet parishioners who claim to have seen the Virgin. If they were all true, she would have to travel widely and endlessly, so we accept the accounts, praise the witnesses for their devotion to Mary, and say no more about it. But when the Don saw that I was trying to use that strategy with him, he took my arm roughly and said: "But I did see her. Come to the room where Inés died." When I stood there he went to a corner and said with the greatest reverence: "She appeared in this corner, right through the solid wall. For that door was closed and I could see the windows. She walked from here where I'm standing to where you stand."

' "Did she touch you?" I asked, and he said: "No, but she did take Inés in her arms. I saw her do it, and before she died, Inés told me: 'I'm going back to the arms of Mary.' She was here in this room, bringing comfort to us."

'What did you make of the story?'

'The usual village sighting, except for one thing. When the Don sought a statue of Mary, the one you see through that window, he searched for a sculptor he could trust and told the man: "I want you to carve her just as I saw her," and he struck a pose for the man that duplicated what he thought he had seen during her visit. And there she stands, just as he described her.'

I remained at the window for some time, staring at Don Cayetano's Virgin, and she did indeed look as if she were protecting the entire village of Mota, but as I reached this conclusion Father Eduardo said: 'I was so shaken by the Don's religious fervor that I went to visit the sculptor to ask if he had seen anything strange about his customer, and he told me: "He was crazy, like the people they used to keep in cages. Because he kept telling me as I worked: 'She held her head this way,' or 'When she bent down to embrace my wife her face had this kind of expression,' and all the time he watched me work he posed this way or that to show me how she looked in real life. And then I knew he sometimes drank too much."'

'But what did you think, Father?' and the priest replied in a manner that told me he wished no further conversation: 'That some men and women of great devotion have a strength greater than yours or mine.'

After my interview with the priest I believed that I had achieved a rounded portrait of my man, and a cable from my editor in New York had confirmed this: 'Shenstone: We think you have the Don nailed down. Paternalistic country squire. Respected by his neighbors. Loves bulls. Has an abiding faith in the Virgin Mary. Struck by a double tragedy, and doomed to see his taurine empire crumble despite heroic efforts to save it. Powerful story.'

Now, as we reached the area in Seville where the barefoot penitents gathered on Palm Sunday morning to drag their wooden crosses in the procession, I was about to plunge into the first of a bizarre series of linked phenomena which I can't explain and which indicated that I had not yet fully understood the depth of Don Cayetano's character. I saw only a few faces I recognized—a couple of generals and town hall functionaries—but even when I nodded to them they

ignored me because they were already in a kind of trance. When three priests came out from the cathedral to bless the marchers, I noticed that Don Cayetano asked each one for his benediction. After the third priest added his blessing to the march, Don Cayetano raised his face upward as if appealing to heaven for some kind of special acceptance, and in this posture he began his procession with his cross dragging behind him.

He had marched for the better part of an hour, halting now and then for me to give him water and the towel I carried, so I was standing not far from him when the first extraordinary event occurred. We were near one of the small churches whose float would be going out that evening, and when he saw the beautiful Virgin who adorned it he suddenly fell to his knees and pleaded: 'Blessed Virgin! Grant me one boon! Help the man who loves you so deeply.'

I cannot describe exactly what happened next— perhaps it was a flash of morning sunlight, but suddenly the Virgin's face was suffused with a golden aura that hung about her head like a halo and a strange light bathed the round face of Don Cayetano, giving it an almost beatific cast. Nothing was said, but I could see that he had interpreted this light as a signal that she had heard his prayer and responded encouragingly. The light faded. The penitents resumed their march.

That night when we were at the Mota ranch, with its owner exhausted from his labors as a penitent, he abruptly resumed his analysis of what a perfect afternoon in a major arena would be if one were mysteriously in command of a string of six bulls: 'You wouldn't want it to be a series of perfect fights, each a duplicate of the others. Maybe the second and sixth bulls would be the exemplars, the ones they would talk about forever.'

'That would leave the first matador with a bad afternoon, wouldn't it? I mean, if he didn't get one of the good ones when he's maybe the best matador of the lot?'

'Oh no! You misunderstand. All six would be honorable bulls. He'd be able to do with one and four whatever his talents allowed—great cape passes linked together, excellent work with the muleta. He'd not be left out.'

'I've noticed that you often talk about linked passes, as if they were the ones that count.'

'They do. In life, Mr. Shenstone, no matter what we're doing, we so rarely get three or four episodes linked together meaningfully, one building beautifully on the other to a proper climax. A businessman has three bold successes, then falls flat on his face. A housewife bakes three cakes and the fourth falls flat on its face. My ranch foreman has two exquisite daughters, lovely brides and mothers, but the third is a whore in Lisbon. In the bullring the same. Two fine passes but the damned bull will not turn for the third. He simply will not turn, and the magic is lost.' Shaking his head, he said grimly: 'When I'm the bull, three perfect passes, then four, then if the matador is equal to it, five. The band plays. The photographs would last a hundred years.'

When I said that five passes like that would be worth photographing, he told me: 'There's to be a special fight in Málaga on the Sunday after Easter. Can you join me?'

'That's what I'm here for. I learn from seeing your bulls in action.'

'I wish they were from the old stock. Our ranch dueled with Veragua and Concha y Sierra to determine who was best in Spain. Often we won.' Apparently those memories were painful, for he changed the subject. 'This may sound . . . what? Maybe insane? Maybe the folly of an old man dreaming of the past? But I will do anything to restore the honor of our family name.'

'Like what?'

'Late Thursday afternoon, when the bullfighters' float leaves its church in Triana for the procession through the streets, I've volunteered to be one of the men who carry it on their backs. Double penance. The cross this morning. The float on Thursday.'

'You're trying to build a linked chain of good deeds to assure your bulls good luck?'

His round face dropped into an almost ugly glare: 'Never say good luck! I do these things for heavenly response. I do not believe in luck. I believe in the intervention of the Virgin Mary on behalf of those who serve her.'

I accepted the rebuke, kept my counsel to myself, and used the offending phrase no more, but I did think that if ever there was a man in need of some good luck, it was Don Cayetano.

On Thursday afternoon when the float of the bull-fighters was scheduled to begin its procession through Seville, he had his driver take us across the Guadal-quivir River and into Triana, where the car stopped in front of the colorful little Church of the Toreros. Several dozen men in work clothes lounged near the church's float with its depiction of the dead matador, and Don Cayetano spoke with them: 'May I help you carry your float?'

'You're an old man. The burden would kill you.'

'I'm Don Cayetano Mota, of the bull ranch, and I must do penance.'

Upon hearing his name, the men, most of them aficionados of the Triana matadors, gathered about, and one man said: 'But the papers told us you already carried your cross on Palm Sunday.' He explained: 'My bulls need whatever help they can get,' and the men laughed but he did not.

He and I went into the little church from which the Virgin had already been taken to be the reigning queen

on the float, and at the spot she had vacated he knelt and prayed for a long time in words I could not hear. At the end he flung his arms in the air and cried: 'Holy Virgin! One boon!' His voice echoed in the emptiness and I was about to rise when from the vacant spot came a woman's voice as clear as the Angelus sounding over the dewy fields of morning: 'I hear you.' That I heard these words there can be no doubt.

Looking around quickly in the church to see if there might be someone else who had heard what I believed I had, I caught a fleeting glimpse of a bent old woman with a black shawl covering her head who must have been seated near the door in the rear. In a medieval romance she would have been described as a crone or, more poetically, a beldame. I was eager to question her but had no opportunity, for as I moved toward her she fled from the church with an alacrity that surprised me, and I wondered if she had heard something of such significance that she was impelled to share it with her neighbors.

Disappointed that I had lost her, I returned to where Don Cayetano sat as if in a trance and I tried to question him regarding the mysterious voice. But he refused to speak, so I was left in a state of bewilderment. Deciding to leave the Don alone with his prayers, I turned toward the door at the back of the church and saw entering breathlessly, as if she had been running, the kind of woman men do not forget: about thirty, tall, with flashing eyes that seemed to throw sparks and with two braids of raven-black hair that reached down to her waist. Her dress was as dramatic as her figure: a colorful shawl about her shoulders, a brilliant green bodice tightly fitted at the waist, and a skirt that flowed down to her toes, where the hems of several lace-trimmed petticoats were visible. I recognized this as the traditional costume that Gypsy fortune-tellers adopted when they moved into a city. Hers was embellished by an upright tortoiseshell comb in her hair and a pair of huge, glistening earrings.

What I noticed most as she pushed open the wooden door and ran into the church was the grace of movement, the elegance with which she drew her right hand to her cheek as if apologizing for having intruded upon us. But this courteous gesture did not prevent her from coming near us to satisfy her curiosity about the two strangers. She turned to study Don Cayetano with special care, then walked boldly past us, flashing a dazzling smile, and left the church, her swirling petticoats brushing my leg as she went past.

Now I had to interrupt the Don: 'Who was that?'

'Some Gypsy. Couldn't you see by her dress?'

'Why did she rush in here to spy on us?'

'Didn't you see the old woman watching us? And leaving in a hurry to warn the Gypsy?'

'But why did the Gypsy run over so fast to spy on us?'

'It's their church, you know. They come to worship here, too.'

Since it was now only a short while before the bullfighter's float would start its sacred journey through the streets of Seville, we left the Virgin's church to mingle with the crowd that had gathered to serve as her guard of honor. As we idled there, surrounded by Gypsies, I scanned the crowd to see if the woman who had spied on us was among them, but I did not find her.

Because I was now so much closer to the statue of the Virgin than I had been before, I realized for the first time how beautiful she was in her dress of heavenly blue with its simple adornments in gold. While admiring her I recalled the handsome color plates in my college text on Renaissance art that showed the Virgin as Regina di Cielo, the Queen of Heaven, and she had been garbed like this. Suddenly I saw something that astounded me. She was cross-eyed! Yes, the peasant sculptor who had carved her two centuries earlier had made her slightly cross-eyed, her right eye looking straight ahead while her left wandered.

Nudging Don Cayetano, who was talking with the group of muscular young men who would be carrying the float, I said: 'Am I crazy, or is she cross-eyed?'

To my surprise he turned away from the bearers, smiled warmly and said: 'Yes, the faithful in Triana call her La Bizca, our word for—' and with forefingers pointing at each other in front of his face, he gave a surprisingly accurate depiction of crossed eyes.

'The Gypsies love her for her human weakness. They say: "She keeps her eyes crossed so she can

squint down the crooked alleys of Triana to see where poor women might need her help." Men, too, I suppose.' When I looked at her again, with that explanation in mind, I saw that she was indeed a flawed peasant girl from some country village near Seville whom a reverent rural sculptor had used as a model two hundred years ago, and in that moment of recognition she became a human figure I could love.

'The girl who posed for the statue—what happened to her? Did she ever marry?'

'I don't know. But *bizcas* make wonderful wives,' the Don said. 'They're so grateful that someone has wanted them. One of my uncles married a *bizca*. He called her his little jewel.'

When the time came to hoist the heavy float, a large group of men, towels wrapped about necks and shoulders, ducked under the apron, and their captain, who remained outside, was about to give the signal to raise the float when one of the men called to Don Cayetano: 'Since you need all the help you can find for those bulls of yours, come on in. You don't need to carry.'

'I must carry,' he said as he disappeared behind the curtain.

The width of each float was limited by the dimensions of one of the notable streets in Europe—Sierpes, the serpent, an extremely narrow alleyway leading out of Seville's central plaza. Converted centuries ago into a street of elegant shops, silversmiths and popular corner cafés, it represented the heart of the city and, some said, of all Spain. None of the magnificent floats that ventured out during Holy Week could consider their citywide transit complete if they did not move through Sierpes. This required exact maneuvering, accomplished by a system of signals to the bearers who could see nothing. The captain of the float remained outside to judge when his men should rest, resume marching or change direction. He did this by slapping the boards to give instructions. A watcher in the plaza who often worked under the float of his church told me: 'One slap means "Pick it up!" Two slaps, "Move off straight ahead!" Three slaps—and we sure like to hear them— "Put it down!"'

As our Triana float neared the narrow entrance to

the famous street I heard the captain shout to his team below: 'Entering Sierpes! Careful, careful!' and with that he gave three resounding slaps, indicating that his men could put down their heavy burden and refresh themselves with drinks and cool towels. It was during this pause that I made my move.

Don Cayetano's decision to participate struck me as so bizarre, especially for a man of his age, that I wanted a photograph of him naked to his waist and mingling with the workmen. I was no photographer, but I was sure I'd manage with the high-speed camera my office had provided. I asked one of the sweating carriers: 'Can I slip in with you? Take some pictures?'

'No light,' he growled.

'But if I gave you—' When he saw my handful of pesos he said amiably: 'For pesos I'll sell the float,' and without explaining to his fellow bearers, he helped me to slip under the heavy float, which was resting on its four wooden legs.

There I found myself in a kind of medieval hell. The men were grimy, sweaty and smelly, laughing among themselves as they drank from leather flasks containing the brutal red wine of the countryside. They were powerful men who had easily adjusted to having Don Cayetano among them. Assuming that I had come to photograph them, they made faces as I swung my camera toward them while they crouched under the float, and in the confusion I was able to catch four or five excellent shots of Don Cayetano as he knelt among them, flexing his shoulders in preparation for the culminating march along Sierpes. 'He's a sturdy old buzzard,' the men told me. 'He carries his share.'

Having taken my pictures, it was my intention to slip out from under the float before it started into Sierpes. But my timing was bad and while I was still trapped inside I heard the slap directing the men to lift the float and get going. The men, realizing I was trapped, laughed at my discomfort and indicated that since I was now one of them, I had damned well better help them carry. Shouldering my camera, I accepted a position two behind Don Cayetano, from where I heard him praying as before: 'Blessed Virgin, let me restore the dignity of my name. Please, please allow me this one chance.'

I cannot say whether the other men toiling in the dark saw what I saw next, but from the spot directly below where the statue of the Virgin stood above us, the boards separated several inches for just a moment, probably caused by the twists and turns of Sierpes. Perhaps I was affected by the heat and stench of sweaty bodies, but I saw the figure of the Virgin herself, suffused by the nimbus I had seen before, slip down through the opening. Bending down, she came directly to the side of Don Cayetano and there in the darkness touched him so that the light that bathed her also graced him. Grabbing my camera, I tried to photograph this astonishing sight, but my doing so must have irritated her, for in that moment she vanished. The crack in the boards closed behind her, and I found myself photographing nothing. Don Cayetano, straining from the weight on his shoulders, made no gesture to indicate that anything unusual had happened, but I know what I saw.

When our float resumed its route up Sierpes to the reverent applause of all who watched, for our cross-eyed Virgin was one of the most cherished in the

Seville parade, Don Cayetano and I exchanged no words because we were exhausted. Even at my age the labor was punishing; for him it must have been infinitely worse, but he would have accepted any travail to obtain help in restoring the reputation of his bulls.

I desperately wanted to interrogate him about that strange happening under the float, but when he guessed that I was about to do so he edged forward, his shoulders bowed with pain, and refused even to talk to me. Only after we had climbed out from under the float, and were washing ourselves with the water and towels provided by women from the church, did he say: 'That was a worthy experience. You'll remember it.'

'What was it I saw in there?' I asked, but he diverted me by taking my arm and pointing up the street to a place I'd often read about in bullfight magazines but had never seen. On the whitewashed wall of a low building some self-appointed artist had used garish colors to paint a sign marking a famous taurine bar. When I saw it I had to laugh, for it proclaimed in black letters EL GALLITO, The Fighting Rooster, below which appeared a fancifully drawn rooster in a red bullfight uni-

form giving a pass to a tremendous black bull. It was a sign that would encourage any aficionado to enter.

As soon as Don Cayetano led the way in, I realized that this was one of Spain's famous tapa bars, for arranged along the front of a bar made of scrubbed light wood were many platters filled with the delicacies of Spain—anchovies, pickled walnuts, quail eggs, roasted peppers—intermixed with dishes loaded with the rural staples of Spanish cuisine, such as massive potato omelettes, chunks of braised oxtail, cheese, ham slices, pieces of roast chicken and piles of chewy peasant bread. A Spanish tapa bar is one of mankind's inspired inventions and an irresistible place for drinking flagons of dark beer.

But El Gallito had a special enticement, for it was also a taurine center, with its smoke-stained walls covered with dozens of photographs of past matadors in their moments of glory: Cuatro Dedos, who killed superbly despite the loss of a finger on his right hand; Cagancho, the praying mantis from Triana; Juan Belmonte and Joselito, the immortal pair; Pepe Illo, the shadowy great from the 1700s; Chicuelo, who invented the delicate passes; Manolete and the Mexican Arruza, who created their own age of glory and who both died young. All these and their brothers of the bullring lived again in this gallery of greatness, but visually, as was proper, they yielded first place to the horned heads of notable bulls who had fought in Seville: the stately Concha y Sierras, the deadly Miuras, the huge Pablo

Romeros and, yes, even three Mota bulls who had been brave—in times past.

Color was provided by the evocative bullfight posters from the last century, designed by fine artists and handsomely printed in colors that had not faded despite time and smoke and even grease from the row of fifty hams suspended from the ceiling, where in the course of one or two years they would ripen in the smoke to become one of the delicacies of Europe.

To stand at the tapa bar in El Gallito with a mug of dark beer, a small plate and a toothpick to spear tempting morsels was to become immersed in both the past and present of Spanish bullfighting. When we sat down at a table, men who had seen the disgraceful fight at Puerto de Santa María stopped by to criticize Cayetano for having sent such inferior animals to the important fight. They made him cringe, but others of better humor came to wish him well, men of the lower class who rarely had enough money to pay their way into a bullring but who knew bulls and matadors. 'Buena suerte, good luck, *Don Cayetano, con sus toros en La Maestranza.'* If he summoned the courage to smile at such visitors, they lingered at our table to talk about bullfighting, and their comments showed they were amazingly knowledgeable.

As I studied the bar and its posters one feature saddened me: the only patrons of the bar seemed to be men, and I thought that with no women allowed the place is losing half its appeal, but that was the Spanish custom. But while I was thinking about this, I was surprised to see sitting at a table in the far rear the handsome Gypsy woman who had come into the church to spy on us. A patron at the bar, supposing that I was the usual American tourist, told me in broken English: 'That one, señor, she is Magdalena, fortune-teller. All bullfighters come here, day of fight, give her coins for good fortune in ring.'

As I stood to move toward her table, the Don whispered: 'I recognize her now. She's Magdalena, older sister of Lázaro López, and just as evil as him.' Having warned me, he stayed at the table, for he did not care to associate with anyone from that infamous family.

'You are most welcome here,' came a soft voice

from her table as I approached. 'I can tell you many things, Mr. Shenstone.'

I stopped cold, startled by the sound of my name in this place: 'How do you know my name?'

'It is my job to know many things, Mr. Shenstone. When I see you and Don Cayetano entering the church across from my home, it is my duty to find out who you are, writing gentleman from New York. Sit down.'

Two Gypsies who had been talking idly with her rose, leaving the table to Señorita Magdalena and me, and as I joined her my first impressions were reinforced: she was certainly very handsome, taller than usual for a Spanish woman and not at all the stereotypical Gypsy of legend. Close up, she was a most attractive woman, and I could not accept Don Cayetano's judgment that she was evil.

'Why do you bother, Mr. Shenstone, to write about Don Cayetano? Surely you know that his ranch has lost whatever glory it may have had.' She pointed over my head to three Mota bulls on the wall: 'In the old days, yes. Today, we weep for his collapse.'

'Are you really Lázaro's sister?'

'I am. And he will reinforce what I said. He'll tell you how bad the Mota bulls are.' Placing her hand on my arm, she spoke as if her one desire was to help me with my story: 'When you went to Puerto de Santa María you must have seen how bad the Motas are.'

'How did you know I was at Puerto?'

'As I said, it's my business to know.'

Before I could query her further her attention was diverted from me by a loud noise at the entrance to the bar, a most improper sound since this was the night before Christ's crucifixion. The man entering the bar was Lázaro López. Tall, grotesquely thin, with a mop of jet-black hair, flashing smile and the imperial manner of a king, he masked in public life, where he was adored, the cowardice he displayed in the ring, where he was so often excoriated. He was a man I did not like, and I knew that Don Cayetano detested him.

López, aware of the Don's hostility, snapped his head back when he saw the rancher and, instead of ignoring him, went directly to his table, where he greeted the Don with a warmth so effusive that it was laughable to anyone who was aware of recent bullfight history. In a voice loud enough that I could hear he cried: 'My dear friend, Don Cayetano, creator of those fabled bulls of Mota! May you continue to have great luck with them at Málaga and Seville, where we shall be meeting again.' His manner and the way he uttered the oily words were so insulting that I wanted to rush over and hit him, but had I done so I'm sure he would have deftly sidestepped me as he did any dangerous bull and delivered a coward's fist from the side when I wasn't looking.

Don Cayetano saved me from such a humiliation by smiling at the matador and saying with the grace of a Spanish grandee: 'Maestro, may you cut ears and tail in your next fights, especially if you do so with my bulls.' The adversaries saluted each other, and the matador moved on, surrounded by his sycophants.

Any knowing aficionado would have recognized that Don Cayetano's wish of ears and a tail to a coward like López was a sardonic jest, and several older men snickered appreciatively within hearing of the matador. Stung by the affront, he turned and glared at Don Cayetano with hate, as if to say: Beware, old man. If you were one of your pitiful bulls, I'd kill you right now. To underscore his hatred he threw an obscene gesture at the old man. Placing his right thumbnail under his big white teeth, he flicked it right in the Don's face, an act equivalent to the challenge to a duel.

Don Cayetano rose painfully to his feet and, facing the matador, threw the gesture back at him. Each knew there could henceforth be no reconciliation. Don Cayetano, honorable breeder of fighting bulls, had accepted the enmity of the matador and issued his own challenge, and I wondered what the outcome would be.

Now the lanky matador, seeing me sitting with his sister, elbowed his way noisily to our table and shouted: 'Writer of lies! You have no place in this bar. Get out!'

His sister cried: 'Lázaro! This one is a gentleman. No!'

The matador was about to grab my arm and expel me, but his sister protected me: 'He has a right to stay here. He knows bulls. He knows you.'

'He has come to make a hero of Don Cayetano. He's a fraud—a fool,' and ignoring his sister's pleas he ushered me away from Magdalena's table. Don Cayetano and I retired from the field of battle and left the tapa bar to the jeering matador.

WHAT HAPPENED on the next day, Good Friday, proved that Seville was justified in its claim as one of the world's most devout cities, on a par at least for this one day with either Rome or Mecca. Since everyone was aware that on this day Christ was crucified, the citizens tried to replicate what must have happened in Jerusalem that Friday in the year A.D. 30.

Relying upon the account given by Saint Luke, they read:

> And it was about the sixth hour, and there was a darkness over all the earth until the ninth hour . . . and he gave up the ghost.

Spaniards had interpreted the sixth to ninth hours to be late in the afternoon till dusk, and when those solemn hours came, the devout imagined their sky to be darkened during those terrible three hours of agony when Jesus hung on the cross. Little movement occurred in the city, for many tried to share Christ's pain and would have assaulted any who broke the somber silence.

The quiet became more intense as the darkness deepened and the hour of Jesus' death drew near. Old men and women, themselves close to death, whispered: 'He is on the Cross,' and 'How terrible it must have been,' and others replied in hushed tones: 'But he did it willingly, to save us.' The old were deeply comforted by knowing that when they died they would be in the arms of Jesus.

I roamed the quiet streets and at dusk dined in silence with the Don. At the end of the meal he said simply: 'She stood at the foot of the Cross and tended his body when the Roman soldiers took him down. She could see the wound in his side, the nail holes in his palms, the points at which his legs had been broken. Her agony must have been greater than what any of us will ever know. Little wonder we love her and cherish her for the pain she suffered in our behalf.'

I was about to correct him about the breaking of legs, for I knew from Sunday school classes that Saint John said specifically that the Roman soldiers broke only the legs of the two thieves who were crucified beside Jesus: 'But when they came to Jesus, and saw that he was dead already, they broke not his legs.' However, I decided not to mention this bit of trivia when I saw that the Don was in a kind of trance, speaking to some spirit or force that I could not see. His voice trembling with emotion, he said: 'You must have suffered when you saw what they had done to the body of your son. My heart breaks with pity for you.' And he wept.

Saturday was spent in solemn reflection, but on Easter Sunday everyone rose early, for Saint Luke had said of the friends of Jesus: 'Now upon the first day of the week, very early in the morning, they came unto the sepulchre where they found it empty. For Jesus had resurrected and risen to heaven.' The citizens of Seville, assured that he had been reborn, spent the day in quiet rejoicing and in meeting with their families.

The passions of Holy Week exhausted, Don Cayetano and I left Seville and returned to his ranch, where we rode out on horseback to the tree-lined pastures where the fighting bulls grazed. I found it almost terrifying to be riding close to four bulls, each of which weighed nearly half a ton, even though they remained indifferent to my presence.

But the Don reassured me: 'If you remain on your horse, they think you are a horse, someone like them, and they ignore you. But if you got down they'd see you as a strange two-legged enemy, and they'd gore you with those long horns.' Being so close to those powerful and deadly animals that I could even smell them helped me to understand these beasts. It was an Easter present I had not anticipated.

THE WEEK following Easter was a quiet time in Seville. It was as if the solemn tragedy of the mournful days between Good Friday and Easter Sunday had so agitated the religious populace that it would require a week to recover. But even during this quiet period the Don could not afford to remain idle. His ranch was under obligation to provide two strings of first-class bulls, one to Málaga for a Sunday fight, the other to Seville for the following Sunday. The ranch's reputation for the ensuing season would depend on what happened on the two occasions; if the catastrophe at Puerto Santa María was repeated at Málaga and a week later at Seville, he might have to go into hiding, so great would be his humiliation.

We therefore spent Monday and Tuesday at the Mota ranch assembling with extreme care the two sets of bulls, and I appreciated the Don's strategy: 'I mustn't make the mistake of thinking that only Seville is important, just because its feria is known everywhere in Europe. If we have a bad day in Málaga they will boo us in Seville before the fight even starts. So let's be sure we get the best animals possible for Málaga.'

It was a privilege for me to learn what a historic bull ranch the Mota was. Starting sometime around 1785, a strain of bulls called the Vázquez was identified as producing the finest animals available. Manageable in size, they had several distinguishing characteristics: outstanding courage, big, smooth bodies, well-formed horns, legs well positioned for driving against picadors' horses and a remarkable propensity for following the cape or the muleta rather than the man. They became almost the prototype of the fighting bull and dominated the plazas during the nineteenth century, when Vázquez bulls from the duke of Veragua's ranch were notable. In the early twentieth century the great bulls from Concha y Sierra upheld the honor of the Vázquez strain, and now Don Cayetano's Mota ranch, among other notable ones, represented the breed.

'I'm not allowed to fail,' he told me as we rode on horseback through open fields where hundreds of animals roamed unfenced. 'When the public sees one of my bulls they see not me but the honorable reach of history.'

When I asked how it was possible to herd fighting bulls in unfenced fields, he laughed: 'Left to themselves, by themselves, my bulls are never dangerous. See, we ride freely among them, but only as long as they remain in a group. If we were to corner that fine fellow over there and keep him away from his friends he'd tear us and our horses apart in his anxiety to rejoin them.' And then he revealed why a matador was able to fight such a powerful animal: 'These bulls, after they are calves, are never touched by man, never fought, never shown a cape. They're pure animals, unsullied so that when they meet a matador in the ring, they do not know him as an enemy, so they follow the cloth, not the man. But they learn fast, and if the fight goes on too long, they'll peg the man, not the cloth, so the matador has limited time to subdue his bull. If he delays he dies.'

Continuing his fascinating account, he remarked bitterly: 'I say my bulls are uncontaminated by men or their tricks. But sometimes Gypsy boys from Triana sneak into my fields at night and with assistance from the moon and the use of a red tablecloth they fight my bulls in secret. Twice we found the boys' bodies when the sun rose. We try to stop them, but it's useless. The great Juan Belmonte learned his skills on this ranch, in dead of night. So did Lázaro López. He should be grateful to me. He stole the use of my bulls to become a matador.'

When I admired one sleek animal feeding off to himself, Cayetano told me: 'That's the kind of bull we picked in past centuries when arenas gave exhibitions, Spanish bull against African lion, or tiger maybe, to prove which was braver. Mota bulls won every time. Gored the African animals and tossed them in the air. That one would do the same if put to the test.'

On Saturday he and I drove to Málaga, that handsome Moorish-styled city on the Mediterranean to stay in an old hotel frequented by the bullfighting fraternity. The three matadors who were to fight the next day were the same we had seen in Puerto de Santa María, but they remained secluded, surrounded only by their own entourages and supporters. Don Cayetano, to my surprise, strove to make himself available to everyone, especially to members of the press. I knew that he found it distasteful to sit in a public lobby and greet strangers, but, as he said, he was fighting for his life, and I listened as he told newsmen: 'I think you'll find the bulls

I've brought to Málaga the finest our ranch has offered in many years.'

'Didn't you say the same about those you sent to Puerto de Santa María?'

'I did not. Those were the first of the season. We hadn't identified them yet. These will surprise you.' Then, as if loath to let the newsmen go, he quickly added: 'These bulls can be fought and you'll find them exactly suited to the matadors.'

'Even López? We hear you had words after the float returned.'

'When Lázaro López gets himself a good bull, he knows what to do with it, and tomorrow he'll have one of the best. Cut an ear, maybe.' It was painful to see this fine man lowering himself in his fight to protect the reputation of his ranch, and I found myself praying, like him, that his bulls would be good.

Early Sunday morning we went to Mass in an old church near our hotel, and he remained on his knees a long time praying audibly. I could not understand his words, but they were impassioned and directed not to the Lord or Jesus but to the Virgin. When the priest came forward to dispense the holy wafer, the Don reached forward like a hungry dog, so eager was he for any dispensation that might aid him on this critical day.

The Don urged me to watch the sorting of the bulls, a colorful ritual that had originated hundreds of years ago when the senior peons of the three matadors who were to fight later that day met to agree upon how the bulls should be paired so that no matador would get the two best or the two worst. It was one of the incorruptible features of the bullfight; all others were susceptible to chicanery or even near-criminal activity, such as shaving horns to disarm the bull, dropping bags of concrete on their backs to weaken them, slyly substituting three-year-olds and calling them mature four-year-olds, and so on through a multitude of evil tricks. At the sorting, honor prevailed: three peons, each as learned in taurine ways as the others, each as eager to protect his matador, tried to compose three pairs as evenly matched as possible. I enjoyed hearing the arguments regarding the bulls identified by the numbers branded on their flanks: 'Two has what might be a bad right eye. Let's pair him with Five, who seems the best of the lot.' When that was agreed the next peon said: 'One is going to hook to the right. I say we pair him with Three, who looks fine.' When that judgment was fine-tuned to Six and Three, the last pair was obvious: One, who might hook to the right, with Four, who appeared superior.

The peons *had* to be honest in the pairings. After the pairings had been completed the numbers were written on three pieces of paper—Two-Five, Six-Three, One-Four—and hidden in a hat provided by the custodian of the ring. Only then did the three peons, in reverse order of their matador's seniority, draw from the hat the pair of bulls their man would fight: this day López got Two and Five, El Viti would fight Six-Three, leaving Paco Camino with One-Four. Each peon, when he reported to his matador waiting in a hotel room, would assure him: 'Today we got the best of the draw. Two bulls just made for you.' While supporters in the dressing room discussed the reported merits of the two bulls, the matador, after discussion with his peon, decided which of his two bulls he would fight first. The graceful Paco Camino said: 'Let's start the afternoon with an explosion. Four, then One.' Like us amateurs who had participated in the sorting, he believed, from reports, that Four might turn out to be the best of the afternoon.

We reached the plaza at shortly after four o'clock, which pleased me, allowing almost a full hour to watch the incoming crowd, to scan the arena to note its condition, and even to roam the back areas where the six picadors were testing their horses and nine banderilleros were stretching their muscles. At about twenty to five the matadors began to arrive: sober El Viti first, of course, for he was a man with a high sense of ritual who felt that he must come early like the matadors of the past. Paco Camino, one of the handsomest matadors of this century though small, appeared next, accompanied by many well-wishers. Finally, in burst Lázaro López in a garish suit of lights fashioned largely of green brocade. He posed for cameras, shook hands with everyone and tested his right leg by lifting his knee and pressing his instep against a railing. He had been gored in the last fight of the preceding year; it had happened, of course, during his futile attempts to kill a bull, a fact that was making him even more tentative and cowardly this year. I suspected that he would be scandalous this afternoon, but hoped that the performance of Camino and El Viti would come up to expectations and would save the day.

At ten to five one of the workmen at the Mota ranch found me among the horses and said: 'Don Cayetano hopes you'll join him in the rancher's box.' I accepted the invitation and was able to see the extraordinary events that occurred while perched on a stool not three feet from the Don.

The first moments of the afternoon were as exciting as ever: the sound of the trumpet, the gate opening and the horseman in eighteenth-century costume riding in to ask permission of the president to conduct the fight, the donation of the key, the gallop back and the opening of the red gates through which the bulls of Don Cayetano would emerge. 'Doesn't this moment grip you?' I asked, but he was awaiting the appearance of his bulls so intently that he said nothing.

The first fight proved that little Paco Camino and the peon who chose his bulls knew something about the animals, for, as they had anticipated, Bull Four proved to be excellent and almost ideally suited to Paco's style. The matador realized this immediately; his peons had run the bull only twice when he saw that the animal followed the cloth as if its nose were glued to it. Hastening to the far side of the ring, he waved his peons away and cited the bull from a considerable distance, holding his big cape firmly by the ends. Moving cautiously forward, one graceful foot almost heel to toe with the other, he suddenly made a vigorous movement with his head, whereupon Number Four charged right at him, but he deftly led the bull off to his left, twisting his cape at the end so that the animal turned rapidly to follow the cape and charge again. Four times this heroic man, looking vulnerable in his resplendent suit, led the bull back and forth, stopping it each time in some magic way so that man and bull seemed linked. The crowd was in ecstasy, for one could come to many fights without seeing such a chain of passes.

At the end of the last series, Paco halted the bull so that its feet were planted solidly, its head swinging and scanning the arena for its next adversary. What it saw was the first picador astride a large horse, and without hesitating, the bull drove at the target with such force that horse and picador came close to toppling backward. But the picador knew his job. Using his long, pointed lance as a prod, he held the bull off with a punishing stab that cut deep into the massive neck muscles. It was a masterly exhibition of the picador's art and should have driven the bull back, but Four refused to retreat. Despite the cruel lance in his neck muscle, the bull kept driving until it succeeded in throwing the heavy horse and its rider to the ground. In a trice the bull was upon the fallen man, stabbing at him four times with deadly horns but miraculously missing him each time by inches. After the fourth unproductive stab, Paco and his peons were able to lead the maddened bull away, and the bullring attendants rushed in to help picador and horse get back on their feet. Both limped from the arena, their afternoon over.

In a normal fight the bull was expected to attack the picadors three times, for this heavy activity was required if the powerful bull was to be slowed down enough to allow a matador to fight him, but on this day

Paco, realizing that this was a better bull than he had seen all the previous year, signaled with a show of bravado to the president: 'Take the picadors out.' This was a daring decision, for the matador was gambling that even though the bull was unweakened, it was such a superior animal that the contest would be more exciting if the animal came to the final segment of the fight in the best condition possible. The crowd roared approval of his gamble.

Pleased that a Mota bull had done so well so far, I said to Don Cayetano: 'Wasn't that the best charge on a picador you've seen in a long time?' To my surprise he made no reply, probably because he did not wish to be distracted from watching as his bull awaited the banderillas that would soon jab into its neck muscles. Paco allowed his peons to place only two pairs because he did not want to make this excellent animal jittery. Now the bull was alone on the far side of the ring, close to our seats, so we had the full advantage of observing at close range the amazing display that now occurred.

Satisfied that he had a great bull, Paco stopped his approach with the muleta at a dangerously far distance, stared at the bull, which stared back at him, and then made the same quick nod of his head that he had used earlier. Nothing happened. Holding in his left hand the drooping red cloth so low it seemed to be waterlogged and with his wooden make-believe sword held tightly behind his back and pointing to the ground, so that it would be totally useless as a weapon of either attack or defense, he took one more step toward the bull, who at this movement thundered forward to attack this insolent creature. It was the moment of maximum danger; before the bull could reach the tantalizing muleta he had to roar completely past the exposed body of the matador, and if ever the bull could have a chance of killing the man, this was it. But with the delicate grace of a master dancer Paco inclined his body so that the bull missed, and at the same instant he gave the muleta a twitch that caused the bull to halt instantly, knowing he had missed the target.

The graceful matador, certain that he had a compliant bull, launched four more passes of such elegance that I told Don Cayetano: 'If the boy manages a decent kill he'll be awarded all the trophies.' The president could award a deserving matador both of the bull's ears, the tail, a circuit of the plaza, and sometimes what Spaniards called a *saliendo en hombros,* the right to depart at the end of the afternoon through the great gates reserved for that honor.

Since I had never before seen a bull that followed the muleta so faithfully, I felt impelled to quote a saying used by true aficionados: 'Your bull is on railroad tracks,' he came and went on schedule—high praise indeed. When the Don ignored me, I saw that he was giving thanks to the Virgin for having been allowed one good bull.

Paco Camino must also have been praying, for with considerable daring he managed a superior thrust that fell short of killing the bull but did bring it to its knees, whereupon a peon rushed out, took his stance behind the bull's still-deadly horns and administered the coup de grâce, a swift short stab at the base of the skull. Since this severed the spinal cord, the bull died instantly and painlessly.

As was to have been expected, as soon as the bull fell a blizzard of white handkerchiefs petitioned the president to award Camino an ear, then two and finally the tail. When Paco's peon had severed *todos los trofeos,* the matador was supposed to hold them triumphantly aloft and circle the plaza. Artist that he was, Paco indicated that his noble adversary who had made the triumph possible should circle the plaza first, and to the uproarious delight of the crowd, the plaza servants, whose job it was to drag away the dead bulls, whipped their mules to a slow run and the fallen bull circled the arena in triumph. When the mules reached the box where Don Cayetano and I sat, Paco ran forward to stop them and insisted that the owner of Mota ranch join his bull in their moment of glory.

To this Don Cayetano assented, and I helped him out of our box as Paco led him to the corpse of the exemplary bull. There the two men saluted the dead animal and indicated to the muleteers that they should resume their march. The crowd cheered ceaselessly, and when the bull finally left the plaza, the matador and Don Cayetano, hand in hand, made one more circuit. I was at the door of our box when Paco delivered him, and I embraced him: 'I have photographs of your tri-

EL VITI
PACO CAMINO
EL CORDOBES

umph, Don Cayetano. In my story all the world will see it. What a climax!'

I was wrong. This was not the climax, for the afternoon had just begun. On his first bull the grave, magisterial El Viti performed the first parts of his fight with somber skill, executing those stately passes of an earlier period that true aficionados prized, and the bull performed so properly that I told Don Cayetano: 'Your bull looks as if he's been hand-tailored for El Viti.'

As the matador prepared for his unique style of killing, I started composing the phrases about him that I planned to use in my report: 'Ten matadors will try maybe once in their lifetime to kill standing perfectly still awaiting the bull but nine out of ten will fail. El Viti, master of the art, will try it every chance he gets and also fail nine times out of ten. The bull hits the sword off to one side. The bull hesitates at the last moment and leaves Viti looking silly. The bull accepts the sword but refuses to fall down. All failures, but for his having tried we honor him.'

Now the moment was at hand when the grave matador, showing no emotion, stood inviting the charge. The bull snorted, plowed the sand with his right hoof and then hesitated, for he had been tricked too often this afternoon. Finally he thrust himself at the sword, which sank deep into his vital organs. With a gasp he fell dead at the matador's feet and the plaza exploded.

Don Cayetano, seeing perfection, shouted: 'Give him ears. Give him everything! Give him the plaza! For he's a man of honor!'

The spectators agreed: two ears, a tail and two circuits of the ring for the dead bull. As before, El Viti stopped by our box and invited Don Cayetano to join him for the parade of honor; when the two men and the bull reached the place where Paco Camino stood watching, they stopped to invite him to join them, and the kind of triumphal circuit ensued that Málaga rarely saw.

In reporting this exceptional afternoon I can hear American and European readers outside Spain saying: 'Two such kills in one afternoon. Too much. Highly unlikely,' but I have twice seen afternoons in which all three matadors cut ears on their bulls, and two also awarded tails. I suspected that this afternoon might prove to be such a day, and when Don Cayetano returned to his box I said: 'Sir, if López gets one of your good bulls, this could be a historic day,' and he replied: 'His first bull's one of the best I've bred. Made for him, but López cannot fight. In the easy parts he's showy. In the dangerous parts, cowardly. Let's pray.'

The breeder was correct in his guess that the first of López's bulls was a fine animal, and once the Gypsy saw that it moved properly, he was, as Don Cayetano predicted, showy. He pranced around the stately animal, almost burlesquing it. He used his cape behind his back and on his knees and while smiling at a pretty girl in the first row. He placed his own banderillas, and did so with grace. The man demonstrated that he was a poet, a ballet master, a sculptor, but even so, he used his fine bull improperly. At the height of his performance, which the less knowledgeable members of the public adored, I said to Don Cayetano: 'Now if he can only do something acceptable with the muleta, we may again hear *dianas.*' I am sure the Don also hoped to hear these evocative chords played when a matador executed a superb move, but he said nothing, for he was praying for the Gypsy to treat his bull properly.

No guardian angel helped us, for in the first half of his muleta work, López was unbelievably coarse. He appeared to be performing the passes that Camino and El Viti had done, but he used his unusual height to keep himself as far away from the bull as possible. At one point I said in a loud voice to Don Cayetano: 'Damn it, he's ruining a fine bull, and he's too dumb to realize it.'

The breeder, who must have been appalled at this humiliation of a decent animal, made no response; he had already told me what he thought of López and saw no necessity to repeat himself.

The nadir of the Gypsy's performance came when the bull, tired and no longer seriously engaged in this burlesque, stood immovable as if to say: Proceed with your nonsense—it's beneath contempt. Knowing the exhausted bull was now safe, López dropped to his knees, stuck his face against the bull's flat, wet nose and kept it there for almost ten seconds. Tourists in the audience were impressed. Having given that display of insolence, he turned his back to the bull while still on his knees and yawned, as if the job of dominating his bulls was boring.

But as in all bullfights, the time came inexorably when he had to kill the bull, and now there could be no escape in sensationalism. Lázaro López was obliged to stand in the plaza alone with a long, slim sword and kill the best bull he'd had in six years. I prefer not to degrade this fine animal by describing how López disposed of him, but the words 'butchery' and 'assassination' come to mind. In the middle of what threatened to become a debacle I said to Don Cayetano: 'That son-of-a-dog should not be allowed in any public place, much less a bullring,' but the Don, heartbroken over this obscene interlude in what should have been an afternoon of unbroken triumph, was too grieved to speak. Only after the bull finally died in shame—the Gypsy's shame—did Don Cayetano say: 'The wrong person died in that ring just now.' I started to ask him what he meant, but now the mules came out at halftime to smooth the sand with drags, and one of Don Cayetano's men came in with drinks.

'That last bull could have been the best of the lot,' the man said, and Don Cayetano agreed: 'Can you imagine what a matador of honor like Diego Puerta could have done with him? Or Mondeño, who practiced his art with such gravity that he quit the ring to become a Dominican monk?'

The next two bulls continued the Mota triumph: Paco Camino cut two more ears and El Viti once again killed *recibiendo,* the only time in recent history any matador had done this twice in one afternoon, and he collected *todos los trofeos*. While I again watched the two triumphant matadors circle the ring together, I said to Don Cayetano: 'It's your triumph, not theirs. You gave them bulls that looked as if they wanted to help. A productive partnership,' but he replied: 'That's expected of a good ranch.' I then said: 'I hope you've provided a good final animal for López, because if he handles it well you and the three matadors will leave this plaza on shoulders.' A few triumphal exits, befitting a Roman emperor, had happened in Spain in recent years, but never after a fight with Mota bulls.

It was not to be. The Gypsy was even more shameful with his second adversary, for as soon as he had to work with the muleta, he complained to the president and the crowd that the bull had been fought before and that it was following him, not the muleta. Assuming the role of a heroic man asked to face an impossible animal, he begged the president to have the bull taken from the ring as unfightable. At this disgraceful appeal, patrons screamed and began throwing things, and now López had just cause to fear attacking his bull with his sword, because a thrown cushion might really imperil him.

But the president rightly refused to allow the fight to end in that manner, and by telephone from his high box he instructed his agent supervising the ring to inform López: 'You kill the bull or go to jail for forty days.' Since that would eat into the heart of the season and cause him to lose half his earnings for the year, López summoned up what little courage he had, went out among the cushions while surrounded by his protective peons, and on the seventh wild attempt wounded the bull so severely that it finally fell down. Quickly the man with the dagger, who had been paid an extra fee by López 'to be special quick on my bulls,' darted out and cut the spinal cord. Don Cayetano turned to me and, in a voice quivering with anger, said: 'That man should be removed from bullfighting,' and I replied: 'I was about to say the same.'

So Paco Camino, El Viti and Don Cayetano were by the cowardice of Lázaro López denied the right they had so richly earned of leaving the ring at Málaga on shoulders. As I trudged out of the plaza I thought: How cruel. The papers tomorrow will headline TREMENDOUS BRONCA AT MÁLAGA, and the story will deal not with the rebirth of Mota bulls but with the fact that the police had to arrest seventeen men who tried to assault the Gypsy torero because of his misbehavior in the ring, and that finally water hoses had to be used to disperse the rioters. Little wonder that Don Cayetano wanted to remove this despicable man from the bullring, but there was no legal way he could do this. The president had sent the order to kill the bull and López had obeyed, in his shameful manner. What was especially galling to Cayetano was the fact that the following Sunday López would again be fighting Mota bulls in Seville.

A VISITOR to the Seville spring feria will retain a precious memory of a spacious tree-lined park with wide, rambling sandy avenues along which the most beautiful women in Europe ride on horseback or in horse-drawn carriages from a past age. Their young men, in the Andalusian dress worn by their grandfathers, prance by on meticulously groomed steeds, and since half the parade moves clockwise and the other half counter, the men meet the same women twice on each circuit. Courtships are often arranged by meaningful glances of the eyes.

Colorful kiosks purvey drinks, sandwiches and candies, and a surprising feature of this almost bucolic scene is the endless number of *casetas,* small and large, tucked under the trees and lining the avenues. Some of these summer houses are splendid affairs, though built only for this brief season. As the riders pass a *caseta* they are apt to rein in their horses and lean down to greet the occupants of the *caseta,* who must, of course, offer *copas* of sherry. At night many of the larger *casetas* employ orchestras, and dancing can last into the dawn. There is no raucous aspect to the Seville feria such as one would find at the great carnivals of Rio or New Orleans or Trinidad; this is a stately celebration filled with grace and memories of old Spain.

Among the finest *casetas* this year was the one belonging to Don Cayetano Mota, for with the extraordi-

nary revitalization of his ranch's reputation at Málaga, he was in a mood to host his many friends who stopped by to congratulate him, to share a *copa,* and perhaps to linger on until the day's roast beef was served wafer-thin on little biscuits flavored with French mustard. Twenty hours a day the Mota *caseta* throbbed with festivity, and Don Cayetano savored each moment, for there had been years when people stayed away from him because the fortunes of his ranch had been so depreciated.

But no matter how enjoyable the merrymaking at his *caseta,* each afternoon at half after four he and I rode into the city and took our seats in the Maestranza to watch that day's fight, but we watched the bulls more than the matadors. With his assistance I was learning to estimate how well a bull would perform from the way he entered the ring and responded to the first capes dragging in the sand. I was not able to detect the irregularities that he could—'He favors his right leg, probably bumped it in the truck that brought him here' or 'That one has a bad eye, very dangerous when it comes time to kill'—but I was beginning to see why

Don Cayetano loved bulls, those from the other ranches as well as his own.

At the Wednesday fight with Murube bulls he told me: 'Great animals, aren't they? Vistahermosa line, rather older than our Vázquez line. The two breeds have always been in competition, regardless of who the ranchers are in a particular period that represent them. That Sunday in Málaga, how we must have made the other Vázquez breeders preen!' For the Thursday fight a special treat had been prepared, a rare appearance of the bulls from the notorious Miura strain. Normally these bulls were reserved for Sunday fights, because their fame guaranteed a gala day, but the Seville feria had sufficient leverage to get the Miuras for midweek fights. Aficionados held these bulls in high regard, for they were the fiercest of all the Spanish breeds, but Don Cayetano said: 'I wouldn't want to breed that line. It's famous only because its bulls have killed so many matadors, including the immortal Manolete. I want my bulls to give every matador a fair chance to display his art. That's been my dream in breeding, a bull of honor who will pull no surprises in the ring—the way a man should stand by his pledged word and not destroy another by a sudden shift in purpose.'

'At Málaga your bulls were honorable. At times it seemed that every bull conducted himself precisely right for that particular matador. The way the big black one allowed El Viti to kill him while standing feet-in-cement. It looked to me as if the bull wanted to die that way, and helped El Viti accomplish it.'

'You're getting a sharp eye, Shenstone!' As he said this I remarked to myself: Strange how forthcoming he is about other people's bulls but how reticent about his own.

Clearly, he was more concerned about caring for his bulls than about discussing them. For he paid fanatical attention to the welfare of his animals. Every morning at dawn, no matter how late the festivities in his *caseta* had gone on, he left his bed and rode across the Guadalquivir to Triana, where he went directly to the Virgin of the Toreros. There he prayed in silence for many minutes, seeking her assistance on the last day of the feria. I accompanied him to the church on Monday and Wednesday—on Tuesday and Thursday I had been too sleepy from reveling—and saw nothing unusual as he implored the Virgin's help in seeing that his bulls conducted themselves respectably. I also studied the little church made famous by the fact that Triana bullfighters came here to pray before their major fights, but made even more famous by the custom that when a Triana Gypsy died in the ring, killed by a fighting bull, his corpse lay in state before this Virgin, to whom he had dedicated his life and his art. To men in the bullfighting fraternity this was a sanctified place, and the marble plaques set into the walls with their florid statements about this or that matador's death lent the church an aura that no other had. In accompanying Don Cayetano to pay his respects to the Virgin, I felt privileged to have been able to share this shrine with the toreros.

On Friday morning, when we arrived just as the sun rose, something happened while Don Cayetano was kneeling in prayer that quite staggered me. I happened to be looking directly at him—bowed head, with hair falling in his eyes in front and bald in back, heavy shoulders, pudgy hands clasped in prayer and held close to his chest—when from her place above the altar I thought I saw the Virgin descend, walk in a stately manner through the sunbeams that filled the church and come directly to where Don Cayetano knelt. Illuminated by the same aura that I had seen underneath her float on Sierpes, she stood over my friend as if bestowing a benediction, and I heard her say as clearly as if she had been speaking to me from a distance of two feet: 'Once more.' At this she turned to go back to her accustomed place at the front of her church, but when she reached it she paused, faced Don Cayetano again and raised her right arm in the gesture of bestowing a blessing. From there, and in a clear voice, she repeated her cryptic message: 'Once more!' and she resumed her wooden image and her position in the niche.

I was afraid to speak of this apparition to Don Cayetano, for he had given no indication that he had either seen or sensed it. If it was merely an illusion of mine because I was so tired, he would not have heard the four words. I studied the scene where this miracle had occurred—I could call it nothing less—and as my eyes roamed the area I broke into laughter, for it was

obvious that what I thought I had seen had been caused by the strong sunlight streaming into the darkened church. It was an illusion, nothing more, and now even as I studied the sun's rays I could see that they made the Virgin seem to be moving again.

But what about the four words? I doubted that I could really have heard them. I had been too generous with my sherry toasts at the Mota *caseta* and was obviously in a euphoric state. More likely, I had become so obsessed, like Don Cayetano himself, with the fortunes of the Mota ranch that I had begun to imagine favorable omens that were clearly unreal. The combination of circumstances—tricks played by the sunlight, the effects of the sherry, the intense preoccupation with the hopes of the Mota ranch—had accounted for what I had interpreted as a miracle. It was brain weariness, that's what it was.

As Don Cayetano and I were about to leave the church, we saw the Triana matador Lázaro López coming in, and as soon as he spotted the Don he leaped at him, grabbed him by the shirt at his throat and cried maniacally: 'I know what you've done, you swine.

You've bewitched your bulls. I don't know how you did it, but you've found the secret.'

I tried to separate the two men because López was much younger and more powerful than Don Cayetano and might have hurt him badly had he started throwing his fists, but to my astonishment the Don did not want my help. Indeed he started to attack López, both physically and verbally: 'You're not a bullfighter, you're an assassin! At Málaga I provided you with the two best bulls of the afternoon. They were perfect. Allowed you to do whatever you wished with them. Didn't you feel the magic, you fool?'

'I did,' López shouted, 'and it terrified me. It wasn't real. No bulls behave with such perfection. When I saw El Viti kill his second while his feet were planted in stone, I knew I was involved in witchcraft of some kind. That bull wanted El Viti to kill him, and so did Paco Camino's. Somehow, you evil old man, you bewitched those animals, and since you hate me, I knew that in the last moments of the last bull, you'd use him to kill me.' Drawing back, López pointed a long finger at Don Cayetano and said in a deep, menacing voice:

'I've discovered your secret, you agent of the devil. You'll not kill me with your witchcraft bulls. Not me!'

'You deserve to die on the horns of a bull, the indecent way you mistreat them—the horrible way you destroyed my two great bulls at Málaga. López, you could have left the ring on shoulders through the great gate if only you'd done your share!'

The matador thrust Don Cayetano aside and growled as he moved forward to pray to his Virgin for success and safety on Sunday: 'I'll see you in Seville, Don Cayetano, you and your evil tricks.'

'On Sunday, then,' Mota said, with a menace of his own. Each adversary stepped back with mock politeness to let the other pass, and the last I saw of López he was kneeling in the exact spot occupied by Don Cayetano only a few minutes before.

ONE OF THE BIGGEST DAYS at the Seville spring feria was the last Saturday, for then older men, who had not been able to participate earlier in the week because of business responsibilities, paraded to give the procession a more stately character. After our early morning prayers in Triana, I rode my own horse alongside Don Cayetano's because I had hired a Spanish photographer to snap some shots of me riding with the subject of my article. I hoped his camera might catch us stopping at one of the more ornate *casetas,* accepting sherry from a señorita dressed in a red-and-gold flamenco costume. One picture like that would epitomize the feria and allow me more space to describe the performance of the Mota bulls.

That afternoon the big event was the first appearance in the Maestranza of fighting bulls from the recently established ranch of the charismatic Peralta brothers, Rafael and Angel, who had grown up near Seville and who fought bulls from horseback. They were an extremely popular pair in Seville, and aficionados who attended the fight would be hoping that their bulls performed well. It promised to be a gala.

When bulls were fought from horseback, a skill that the brothers had perfected, this act in the corrida came first. This distinct art form placed the matador astride a marvelously trained horse with which he performed extraordinary feats of skill and daring, culminating in the moment when, guiding his horse only with his knees, he held aloft two banderillas, rode straight at the bull, leaned far out of his saddle and placed the barbs in the neck muscle of the charging bull, then nudged the horse away from the horns at the last possible moment. It was breathtaking, but not entirely to my taste.

Of course, the horseman would try also to kill while mounted, using a long lance, but this maneuver required such a demanding mixture of horsemanship, skill with the right arm and luck that it was rarely completed. In such a case the horseman dismounted, took an ordinary muleta and sword and dispatched the bull on foot. On this afternoon it would have been improper for either of the Peraltas to fight and kill their own bull, so the assignment was given to the horseman Fermín Bohorquez, who performed commendably. The afternoon was off to a fine start, but the Peraltas' bulls, giving ample evidence that they came from a new ranch, so dispirited the other three matadors that they gave

only perfunctory performances and the affair degenerated into a corrida that produced no ears for the matadors and no accolades for the Peraltas. True aficionados did not lament the disappointing afternoon; they accepted it as the luck of the draw and were consoled by the thought of tomorrow's opportunity to see whether the apparent revitalization of the bulls of Mota extended into a second Sunday. If it did, the fight in Seville could be historic.

The day was so important to the fortunes of Don Cayetano that he did not join the Saturday-night revelry in his *caseta,* nor did I. We went to bed in a back room, rose early and drove across the bridge to the bullfighters' church, where we offered our prayers to the Virgen de los Toreros. Once again in the sunlight the Virgin seemed to smile at him, as if promising that his prayers would be answered. For breakfast we went to El Gallito, and as we approached the bar I chuckled at its colorful sign. Through the years Gypsy toreros about to fight in the Maestranza had stopped by to ask the rooster for good luck. If he helped them perform well, late that night they would come back, salute the tough little fellow and whisper *'Gracias.'* Then they would turn to the church and tell the Virgin: 'We thank you, too.'

Breakfast at El Gallito was invariable: a hard roll toasted and soaked in olive oil and rubbed with garlic, a small *copa* of Machao, an anise liqueur, and perhaps a mug of bitter chocolate so thick you could hardly dunk your roll in it, accompanied sometimes by murderously greasy doughnuts laden with granulated sugar. It was a meal ideally suited for men who spend all day unloading ships docked in the nearby river—not for a magazine reporter—but I had to admit it was delicious.

As we ate, a ragamuffin of ten or eleven came to our table and, after looking about cautiously, said: 'I know you, Don Cayetano. My brothers and I sometimes sneak out to your ranch at night with our muletas to fight your young bulls. They're fine animals and we hope they do well this afternoon.'

Cayetano, who could not be happy to hear that his

bulls had been caped, said gruffly: 'You be careful doing that. You'll get yourself killed. Boys do, you know.'

'You don't take them to the police?' I asked Don Cayetano.

'No,' piped up the boy, 'and that's why we feel good about you, Don Cayetano.' He hesitated, then added: 'That's why I've come to warn you.'

'About what?'

'You yourself may be killed this afternoon.'

Don Cayetano blanched, took the boy by the arm and asked: 'What do you mean? I might be killed?'

The boy drew closer, looked around the café again and said in a whisper: 'It's Lázaro López, he's an ugly man.'

'What about him?'

'We heard him say the other evening—my brother and I clean up this place, so no one notices us—'

'What did he say?'

'He was bragging to other bullfighters—said that on Sunday in the Maestranza he was going to kill you.'

'How was he going to do it?'

'The others asked the same question, but he wouldn't answer. Said only that he had found out your secret. Knew how you did it.'

'Did what?'

'He wouldn't say. Just repeated "I know what he's up to with his bulls," and no matter how many times they begged him to explain, all he would say was "We Gypsies know these things. My sister tells fortunes, you know—she solves riddles." And then he repeated: "Tomorrow that son of a pig"—that's what he called you—"tomorrow he dies."'

The boy had delivered his message to a man he admired and even considered in some strange way his friend, and he slipped away, but Don Cayetano, unwilling to see him go without a reward, told me quietly: 'Run after him and give him this. I want no spies to see me talking with him.' When I caught up with the boy he refused the money, saying: 'I fight his bulls at night. I owe him something,' but I insisted: 'You're a brave boy to fight bulls by moonlight and to come see Don Cayetano with such a message. You've earned the money. Take it.' He reached for it, but before letting him have it I asked: 'López said his sister solves riddles? What does that mean?'

'She's a strange one. A witch maybe. When I was young we were afraid of her, but when my brother's wife was going to have a baby he went to see her and without ever seeing his wife the Egyptian told him: "Twins. One boy, one girl," and that's what came out. People say she sees things others don't.'

'Who is this Egyptian?'

'Magdalena López. She calls herself The Egyptian. They learn how in Egypt.'

'What could she see about today's fight?'

'She and López talked a long time—about Mota bulls, about mysterious happenings in Málaga, and the fight in the church. . . . She told him something—magic and something like that.'

'You think she was serious when she warned her brother?'

'Oh, yes! That one doesn't play games.'

Intrigued, I asked: 'Could I see this Egyptian?' and without hesitating he said: 'You'll have to give money. She tells fortunes, you know.' When I indicated that this would be no problem he said: 'Come along,' and we moved toward the exit. But feeling I could not leave Don Cayetano alone in the bar, I went back and was somewhat relieved to find him surrounded by aficionados with whom he was discussing that afternoon's corrida.

Their interests were professional: 'Tell me, Don Cayetano, how could your bulls have been so rotten in Puerto de Santa María and so excellent in Málaga?'

'When a bull ranch is on its way back to respectability, sometimes the older bulls can be pretty bad, never rotten as you say, but difficult. A rancher like me has to live with that.' Here he smiled expansively: 'But he gets his joy in seeing what his new bulls are doing, and mine are on their way back. This afternoon in the Maestranza you'll see how fine a Mota bull can be.'

'You really think so?'

'I'm convinced of it. If the matadors prove equal to their task, you'll see miracles.'

The men listened in silence, for they respected this old man, even though his fortunes were down at

LA EGIPCIANA

the moment. He was a neighbor, a *compadre,* so they meant it when several of them embraced him: *'Buena suerte,* Don Cayetano.' As I left the group I thought that in Triana it means something to be the owner of a bull ranch, even one like Mota that's been declining.

The boy led me to a typical Spanish cottage opposite the Church of the Toreros, a small whitewashed affair jammed in between two larger ones, also white, all of them encroaching on the sidewalk lining the road that crossed the Guadalquivir into Seville. The house, marked by a colorful sign proclaiming LA EGIPCIANA, had four windows facing the street, each barred with a heavy iron grille to prevent the riffraff from ransacking the place. Other than its sign, it was indistinguishable from a thousand others to be found in the small towns of Spain, but when the boy led me inside I found myself in a unique world, for Magdalena López was an authentic Gypsy fortune-teller, and the room in which she met with her clients exuded an air of sinister mystery. It was dominated by a round table covered by a hand-woven cloth with a fringe that reached down to the floor. On it rested a milky-white globe some twelve inches in diameter. Around the table were four comfortable-looking wooden chairs, and in the only one that had arms sat the woman who had so entranced me at the tapa bar. When she came forward to greet me, her graceful walk made her skirt sway in the most charming manner, and again I was captivated.

The room contained many objects bespeaking her trade: a stuffed owl, a six-pointed wooden star, a deck of cards fanned out and glued to a board, a tall, slim earthenware vase containing a bundle of sticks that

protruded at uneven lengths and colorful chromolitho-
graphs of the pyramids, Luxor and the Sphinx. Shades
were drawn over the grilled windows facing the street,
but the solitary one in the opposite wall looked out on
a garden with flowers.

'I bring an American,' the boy said. In colloquial
Spanish she addressed me: 'I'm a businesswoman. I
will tell you all things, but we go no further, Mr. Shenstone, until you place silver here,' and she indicated a
circle woven into the cloth covering the table. While I
responded to her request the boy said: 'Remember,
Magdalena, I brought him. Something for me, too,' and
she gave him some pesetas. He then turned to me: 'And
you? How would you have found her without me?'
After I too contributed, he ran off, leaving us alone.

As I sat down her comment proved she had continued to monitor the movements of Don Cayetano and
me: 'You continue to visit the Virgin across the way.'
When I nodded, she continued: 'You want to know
about the corrida this afternoon, and I know the
answers.'

'Will your brother do well?'

'Ears and tail.'

'And the other matadors?'

'You're not interested in them. You want to know about the bulls of Don Cayetano.'

'Will they do well?'

'Why not? Under the circumstances.'

'What is it you know about the "circumstances"? Which your brother also seems to know about?'

Taking a filmy red cloth of considerable size, she draped it over the white globe and said: 'It's my responsibility to protect my little brother. Who took him out to the bulls of Mota on moonlit nights? Who counseled him when he was beginning to fight three-year-olds? Who advises him on his contracts, warns him which bulls to avoid, which to look for? Mr. Shenstone, I know far more about bulls and matadors than you will ever know, than most of the managers know.'

'But you haven't told me about this mysterious secret of Don Cayetano's.'

'Nor shall I, but I will tell you this. The widow in

Texas that you've been thinking you might marry—forget her. She's bespoken to another man. And in her place do not court a blonde. For you they are no good.'

'Señorita Magdalena—'

'Señora. I was married twice. First time at fourteen. I've always had the gift of seeing things.'

'And what do you see for this afternoon?'

'Tragedy. This afternoon will be remembered in Seville, but you will not be free to write about it as it actually happens.'

'Your brother? Does he suffer the tragedy?'

'It's my duty to look after my brother.'

She would tell me no more, and when I found myself back on the street I lingered a long time basking in the morning sunlight. What faced me now was an undramatic but enchanting street, with whitewashed houses, cobbled roadways, a tapa bar at the corner, shawled women drifting by, the smell of chicory burning and the muffled tolls of a distant bell. This was the real Spain, the antithesis of the glitter of the feria across the river, and as I started toward the Guadalquivir, which would take me back into Seville, I suddenly realized that I did not want to leave Triana; the answers I was seeking were to be found here in the Gypsy quarter rather than in the bullring itself.

As I stood in the middle of the street I could see to my left the delicate tower of the Church of the Toreros in which I had imagined seeing the Virgin step off her pedestal to respond to Don Cayetano's plea for help; to my right, huddled close to the earth, stood the fortune-teller's cottage, where Magadalena López had instructed her brother when he came for help. The heavens toward which the steeple points, the ancient earth on which the cottage rests, I said to myself. Virgin and Gypsy. The duel between these two is as old as the stones in that bridge before they were dug from earth and cut to size. And it resumes this afternoon. What an uneven contest. The Virgin with all the powers of heaven, the Gypsy with only those fake Egyptian symbols and her animal cleverness. Bowing to the dignity of the church and saluting the Gypsy's cottage, I made my way back to Seville and the sorting of bulls for that day's fight.

As always, Don Cayetano avoided the sorting. I

almost wished I too had stayed away, for three American congressmen on a junket to Spain, brought by a young man from our embassy to see the bulls, learned that I was an American and bombarded me with questions. I supplied them with bits of information about bulls that I'd picked up from Don Cayetano, and when they asked how I'd learned so much, I said offhandedly: 'I'm staying with the man who breeds these bulls.' This led them to ask who I was and I replied: 'A writer. Freelance usually. But this time for *World Sport.*' They'd seen some of my stories and asked to be photographed with me in front of the bulls whose fates were being decided by the matadors' peons.

I hope they kept the photographs, for they were posed with the bull branded 318, name of Torpedo, to be fought that afternoon by the fiery El Cordobés, who would lead him to immortality. If the man who took the photos kept the negative he could earn a pretty peseta selling copies in Spain.

When I returned to the *caseta* I found Don Cayetano alone in his bedroom, and I took the opportunity to ask him about something that had been puzzling me. Somewhat timidly I said: 'Forgive me for prying, but could you tell me why when we're here in the *caseta* or outside chatting with the riders who stop by or when we're in the church you talk freely, but when we're in the box at the fight, you refuse to talk?'

Looking at me curiously, he said: 'I'm worried about my bulls. Praying maybe.' Then he added: 'Hoping they'll perform well.'

'At Málaga it almost looked as if you were consciously willing your bulls to behave this way or that, to give maximum opportunity to the matadors. Especially with those two kills by El Viti. Have you some magical secret about communicating with animals?'

Again he studied me, then smiled: 'It's in the breeding.'

'But what did Lázaro López mean when he said in church that he was going to kill you today?' He was silent. 'And especially, what could that little midnight torero have meant when he told us that López boasted his sister had given him your secret?'

He leaned back and said: 'Strange things happen

in Triana. Gypsies, you know,' and he launched into an amazing yarn about how, some five hundred years ago, the first Gypsy arrived in Spain, on foot, over the Pyrenees. He was an ingratiating fellow who bamboozled the king of Spain into believing that he, the Gypsy, was from the fabled land of Prester John somewhere south of Egypt, where a colony of Christians lived in peril. On specifics the stranger had been cleverly vague; he deemed it best, he said, not to reveal the precise location of the land lest the Muslims hear and decide to invade it. What the Gypsy wanted was funds to gather an army and march through pagan lands to rescue the isolated Christians from Muslim tyranny. For some forty years this interloper lived off the riches of Spain, doing no work and making no effort to collect his liberating army. When either the king or his advisers asked when the invasion was to begin, the Gypsy had a dozen plausible excuses for his delay.

'What finally happened to him?' I asked.

'The chroniclers forgot to say. Most likely he remained in Spain and brought a lot of other Gypsies here with him. I think their invasion started in his time. Been a problem ever since.'

'Do you think Gypsies have secret knowledge? Does López?'

'They all do. Didn't he say his sister had powers?'

'Yes.'

'Well, maybe that's it.' Preferring to answer no more of my questions, he prepared for the crucial afternoon on which the fate of his ranch depended. At four he gravely said good-bye to his friends at the *caseta,* and I noticed that he did so with an emotion that seemed almost excessive because the bullring was not much over a mile away. But, of course, this was an important day. At the plaza, too, he treated the men he had known for many years with the same deep affection: 'Greetings, Don Alvaro, it is truly good to see you. Hello, Domingo, you rascal.'

Well before five we entered the ranchers' box and I paid attention to the cartel for the day. It was promising: The afternoon would start with Diego Puerta, a matador from Seville who was justly revered in the area. He would be followed by the clownish El Cordobés, a tested crowd pleaser, and the afternoon would end with López, darling of Triana, capable of exciting even the most exacting aficionado if he had a good afternoon with a compliant bull. As for the string of Mota bulls, I'd seen them a few hours ago and judged them to be as fine as those we'd had at Málaga, and the afternoon started as it had a week before.

Diego Puerta, highly regarded as the gentleman matador of his era, was textbook-perfect in his performance, never gaudy, never excessively daring, always at the right place at the right time. But again I had the curious feeling that his bull was cooperating with him almost as though he had been programmed, but when I turned to ask Don Cayetano about this, he was again praying to the Virgin, head bowed, hands across his stomach. Puerta gained two ears and in my opinion should have won the tail, too, but plaza presidents in Seville were demanding, as should be the case in Spain's classic arena.

El Cordobés, I must admit, was a wonder, citing the bull from a preposterous distance, much greater than anyone else would attempt, for if the bull charged, he would arrive at the matador with such force as to knock him clear out of the ring. But Cordobés knew his bulls and could judge when it was safe to pull his tricks. Walking boldly in a straight line, one foot directly before the other, he closed on the bull, which charged smoothly at the right moment and allowed Cordobés to perform beautiful cape work. He followed this grand opening with flourishes and, dropping to his knees a fantastic distance from the bull and staying there, challenged the bull until it charged right at him with such force that I thought he was done for. Without shifting his knees, Cordobés swung his cape outward just far enough to lure the bull in that direction. As the bull roared past, inches from the kneeling man, I thought: That's an act of courage I can't even imagine duplicating. That kid must have ice water in his veins.

With the muleta he was brilliant, leading the bull around, as they say, 'like his puppy dog,' and showing the discriminating aficionados of Seville how to respond to a worthy bull. Indeed, at the height of his performance I thought the bull was the hero of this fight.

Those in the stands thought so, too, and Don Cayetano, suddenly alert and observant again just as the bull died, grabbed my arm: 'Magnificent animal. The crowd wants him to circle the arena.' The president agreed with the spectators, and El Cordobés came to our box and led Don Cayetano to walk beside the animal that had performed with such grace and valor.

When El Cordobés finished three turns, López stepped forward to await the entrance of his first bull. There were both cheers and jeers, but the Gypsy was determined to give a good performance before his Triana supporters, and even I had to admit that he was effective with his cape, better with his banderillas, astonishing with his muleta and, uncharacteristically, capable at the kill. This was the Gypsy magician they had raved about when he first appeared on the scene, and he was given both ears, the tail and three circuits of the arena.

Diego Puerta's second bull was *regular*—a wonderful Spanish word with its last syllable drawn out and pronounced *-lahr* to rhyme with scar, which meant 'Not good but not bad, either.' Puerta cut one ear.

For the fifth bull of the afternoon El Cordobés drew No. 318, Torpedo. From the instant the bull entered the plaza and charged straight across the arena, head high, horns cocked to meet any adversary, patrons began to cry: 'Toro! Toro!' and the cries mounted when this noble animal left El Cordobés and his cape and from a surprisingly short distance hit the first picador with such force that the man was thrown down before he could lodge his lance in the animal's neck muscle. From there the bull cantered purposefully to the second picador, whom he also dismounted to cheers. The first picador had now remounted, and this time he protected himself and his horse so that he was able to place one lance, a tremendous blow, which he intensified by leaning forward with all his weight. He then performed what cynics derisively called 'the carioca,' a dancelike trick in which the picador kept his horse's bulky body moving in front of the bull so that the latter could not escape, while the picador continued to lean on his lance and really punish the animal. It was a disgraceful act, but it did aid the matador in reducing the power of a difficult bull; this time it reduced nothing, for the bull was more than able to withstand the extra punishment.

At this point the president, judging that the bull had been tired adequately by the two dismountings—which had required enormous effort from the bull's front quarter and hind legs—signaled the trumpeter to sound the call for the next act with this illustrious animal. Cordobés did not object; recognizing that he had a chance for exceptional work with the muleta, he unfurled a series of such exciting passes, one linked to another, that many in the crowd leaped to their feet shouting 'Toro! Toro!' When Cordobés finished his muleta work with a monumental pass of death, which fixed the bull for the kill, people began crying 'No! No!' The protest became so loud that Cordobés did not prepare to kill but, instead, launched another series of *pases naturales* of such grace that cheers thundered across the plaza, reaching a climax when he daringly tried yet one more pass of death, most dangerous because the bull might remember the trickery from the time before and go for the exposed man instead of the muleta. Not this bull. He drove straight ahead, lifted both his horns and his front feet and came to a dead halt, awaiting the sword, but the protests against killing him became even more vociferous. The president, fearing there might be a riot if he allowed the kill, finally lifted his white handkerchief and signaled that the bull should be spared, to the resounding joy of everyone in the arena.

Five tame oxen, castrated and heavy, entered the ring to rescue the bull and take him out alive. When they surrounded him he sniffed at them, recognized them as brothers from the corrals and the departure was completed, with women throwing flowers before the departing hero. While men near us shouted: 'He was too brave to kill' the Don quietly gripped my left hand and whispered: 'Once more a Mota bull is rewarded with an *indultado*. The assurance of our rebirth.'

In the pause that followed, some spectators began chanting 'Matadors! Matadors!' while others cried *'Ganadero, Ganadero!'* for the breeder, and I helped Don Cayetano rise to join the three matadors as they paraded. It was an honor few ranchers had ever known

in the Maestranza. When the circuits were completed, the matadors returned Don Cayetano to our box, where Puerta and Cordobés, their major work for the day completed, embraced him. Far from making such a gesture, López said venomously in a low voice that only Don Cayetano and I could hear: 'Now we duel to the death. My sister has explained your trick,' and Mota replied in a harsh voice I had not heard before: 'Let it be so. You deserve to die.'

As the fight was about to begin, Don Cayetano again bowed his head and began to pray, and again the Virgin seemed to respond, for the sixth bull performed much like the third, with which the Gypsy had achieved wonders. But then something happened that altered the entire day—indeed, my whole trip to Spain. At the conclusion of a series of cape passes that even I had to admire, López, inspired by some evil genius, stood before the confused bull and humiliated it with a series of gestures intended to denigrate it. When people began to protest, López, holding his cape in his left hand, moved directly in front of the right horn so that it touched his own breast, and then, with a powerful

swipe of his right hand, he beat the bull in the face, repeating the act three times.

'No!' I shouted to Don Cayetano, but his dazed eyes looked as perplexed and sorrowful as the bull's. Soon the entire plaza was booing, and in that instant I realized that López was abusing not the bull but its owner; he had confused the two. 'What did you think of that exhibition?' I asked Don Cayetano, and when he didn't answer I shook him, for this had been a significant moment in the fight, but again he did not reply. Instead his head fell even farther forward and his hands, which I had disturbed in their peaceful clasp, dropped to his side. Supposing with horror that the old man had died, I started calling for help but stopped when I saw he was still breathing and that no external part of his body showed any signs of death. He was not dead, but had he fainted? I slapped him vigorously, but he did not respond. 'What's happening?' I shouted, but no one heard me.

In my confusion vivid images and remembered sounds started to return, tentatively at first, then in a flood. From the fight in Málaga I heard myself saying:

'Don Cayetano, the bulls you gave those matadors looked as if they wanted to help. This one is hand-tailored for El Viti.' Or I was again under the float, with the Virgin coming down through the cracks in the planking to give the Don reassurance. Next I heard the menacing words of Lázaro López as he warned that he had penetrated the Don's secret. Then came the Virgin again, in the church, and her mysterious words: 'I hear you,' and, during the second visit, her cryptic promise: 'Once more.'

As I cowered in the darkness of the box, fighting to make sense of this jumbled evidence, it seemed as if an explosion suddenly blasted my mind, and for the first time I understood how the Virgin and Don Cayetano had conspired to restore the honor of his ranch. Don Cayetano had never been praying when he sat beside me; he couldn't because he wasn't there—he was in the bull! Determined to have his animals do well, he had, with assistance from the Virgin, become those bulls. After his many humiliations he had finally achieved afternoons of triumph; he had circled the plazas with cheering in his ears, and he had seen one of his bulls sent out alive crowned with laurels such as few bulls gather. The honor of his ranch had been restored.

But I was sure Don Cayetano would never be satisfied with gains only for himself. He must also protect the honor of bullfighting, the efforts of all the breeders who had suffered humiliation at the hands of the villainous Lázaro López. The Gypsy must die. And he would be slain by Don Cayetano himself. As I reached this conclusion my mind was filled with a blaze of light in which I saw things clearly. At the climax of the fight Mota, the fat little rancher, the ridiculed one, would drive his right horn deep into the heart of the Gypsy, and do it in full sight of the aficionados of Seville and Triana.

But he must act immediately, for with the conclusion of this fight, the Virgin's obligations to the Don would end. Twice she had listened to his pleas, at Málaga and now in Seville, and twice she had rewarded him with immortal corridas, but I myself had heard her give warning: 'Once more!'

Then I was gripped by a terrible thought: Had Gypsy López somehow, with the aid of his clever sister, penetrated Mota's secret? If so, wouldn't he plan to kill Cayetano before the latter could kill him? Yes, I now remembered his exact words during that confrontation in the church: 'You'll not kill me with your witchcraft bulls.'

When my churning brain cleared, I saw that this weird plot could have only one resolution. Since López and his necromancing sister had surely guessed the Don's secret, the Gypsy had only one escape from those deadly horns—he must kill the rancher before Mota could kill him. Fearing that Don Cayetano might be moments from death, I rushed through the passageway between the fence enclosing the ring and the stands, shouting in Spanish toward the bull: 'Don Cayetano! He means to kill you! Don Cayetano! Leave the bull! López is going to kill you!'

Of course, no one could make anything of the message I was trying to deliver, and before I could get anywhere near where López was finishing his preparatory work for the kill, the officials, thinking that I was one more drunken tourist, halted me and pinned me against the red fence.

López, having given the bull an artistic fight filled with emotion, was assured of *todos los trofeos* if he killed decently, and he must have been tempted to try, but when I saw him put aside the wooden sword matadors used in the first stages of the muleta to take instead that long, curved-tipped steel sword that dealt real death, I saw that his face was gray, not from fear of the bull but from the secret knowledge of what he must do next.

At this moment he spotted me pinned against the fence, and I was close enough to shout: *'No lo hagas, López!* Don't do it!' When he dismissed me with a wan but bitter smile, I tried again to alert Don Cayetano, still convinced that he could hear me: 'Leave now! Now!'

'Let me go!' I shouted at the men holding me, but they feigned not to understand my Spanish, simple though the words were: *'Suelta me!'* Still held back by stout arms, I had to watch impotently as the final act unfolded.

Instead of properly citing the bull, no sooner had López taken the deadly sword from his peon than he ran directly at the bull, swung quickly to the left and jabbed the sword with all his might not through the hump of muscle protecting the spinal column but deep into the fleshy side of the bull and toward the heart itself. The astonished bull, mortally wounded, took two steps forward and collapsed. Before I could scream a warning to the peon running out with the dagger to complete the kill, a tremendous *bronca* erupted, protesting the shameful murder of this great bull. My voice smothered by the cries of outrage, my arms immobilized by the custodians, I stood powerless as the dagger man leaped forward and severed the spinal cord. Instantly, as if by magic, the bull dropped dead, and I wondered in panic whether Don Cayetano had escaped in time.

'Let me go!' I shouted, but no one heard, and by the time my captors released me I had difficulty fighting my way back to our box. The outraged spectators began leaping into the alleyway to thrash López, who was begging the police to protect him, and I wasted precious minutes elbowing my way through the riotous crowd. I had no need to hurry; the foreman of the Mota ranch came running toward me shouting: 'Oh, Señor Shenstone! Don Cayetano is dead. Our day of greatest triumph and he's dead!'

When we finally reached the box a doctor who had been summoned from the crowd pointed to the flecks of blood on the rancher's lips: 'A blood vessel deep inside must have ruptured. You can see he was very fat.' As I looked at his corpse I asked myself: How can I report such a story? and a voice of conscience rebuked me: You unfeeling bastard! Your good friend is dead and all you can think of is how to write about it in your story. For shame!

Only then did I see Don Cayetano as he truly was: a man with two abiding passions, to serve the Virgin and to restore honor to his ranch. He had died in the service of both ideals, and few old men can claim as much.

Kneeling beside the body that still remained in its chair, I straightened his hands, eased his head to one side and whispered: 'Your secrets are safe, Don Cayetano. And your bulls did triumph. Listen to them still cheering outside.' I was lying to the old man, for the noises in the arena came not from spectators cheering that last noble bull but from ragamuffins who were trying to kill Lázaro López, who was creeping out of the bullring surrounded by the police, who had been given their orders five hours before: 'Go to the plaza and protect López if he gives another of his afternoons.'

I was so unnerved that when the hospital crew came to take Don Cayetano's body away, I followed after them aimlessly. I saw the golden sand on which Don Cayetano had paraded in triumph, and the red gate through which his bulls had charged to glory, and then I was out on the streets of Seville, wandering not back to my hotel but across one of the bridges over the Guadalquivir and into Triana, for on this night I wanted to be with the bullfight people.

In a kind of trance I reached the Church of the

Toreros, and when I looked in I saw only three flickering candles lighting the statue so revered by the Gypsies of Triana. She did not see me, for she looked over my head to the back of her church, her cross-eyed smile serene and all-embracing. I knelt before her and prayed: 'Compassionate Virgin, whose crossed eyes see the good and bad in men, guide your faithful servant Don Cayetano Mota through the gates of heaven this night. Pray God to forgive the murderer Lázaro López. These damned Gypsies know no better. And grant me peace of mind, for mine has been badly shaken here in Seville.'

When I left her church I continued on to El Gallito, where the aficionados of Triana in noisy numbers were celebrating the triumphs of their hero, Lázaro López. Standing unnoticed at the edge of the crowd, I could see the handsome Gypsy features of the matador above the heads of his adoring fans, and I noticed that he had one very black eye where some outraged spectator had punched him during the *bronca* that ended his performance.

Unwilling to be part of any crowd that was honoring such a man, I left the bar but not Triana, for I felt compelled to probe the secrets of this mysterious town, and this brought me back to the fortune-telling house of La Egipciana. Although it seemed likely that she would be somewhere in the town celebrating her brother's survival, I nevertheless banged on her door and was gratified when she opened it just wide enough to inspect me by the pale light in the street.

'Oh!' she cried as she admitted me. 'The man whose woman in Texas is betraying him!' and she indicated a seat at the table on which sat the glass sphere, still covered by the red cloth. She spoke first: 'Were you at the corrida, Señor Shenstone?'

'In the box of Don Cayetano.'

'Then you saw everything?'

Cautiously, for I could not guess what secrets she might be willing to reveal, I whispered: 'I saw your brother murder Don Cayetano.'

Betraying no emotion, she reached past me and removed the red cloth from the globe. Appearing to stare into the milky-white orb she said in a singsong voice that I had not heard before: 'We Gypsies are not powerless, you know,' and then she pointed across the street to the Church of the Toreros: 'All the world receives help from that one.'

'The Virgin?'

'Yes, even in America she's available to you. We Gypsies have our own special ways of helping each other. Why do you suppose, Señor Shenstone, that you find me sitting here in the dark on such a triumphant night? Because I know it's on such nights that Gypsies want to talk with me, to ask questions, to give thanks.' She paused, stared into the globe and said: 'I was expecting my brother, and you came along. Maybe that's better. You have difficult questions, don't you?' When I nodded she laughed and, as on our first meeting, I thought: What a handsome woman, what flashing eyes. But I also felt fear, because if she was able to do in that bullring what I was sure she had done—protect her brother from the full weight of heaven—what might she do to me if she became angry?

Seeing that I was fearful, she placed her hand on my arm and said gently: 'Ask your questions, my American friend, but even if you get the answers, they won't do you any good, because you'll never be able to write about them, will you?' When I remained silent, she added: 'Who would believe you?'

'Don Cayetano was in the bull?'

'As a sensible man you must know that would have been impossible.' Then she flashed a condescending smile as if I were a small child: 'Do not try to solve all the mysteries.'

'How did you know so much?' I asked.

'Because I know bulls. Have to if I'm to protect my brother. Everyone knew the Mota bulls had become no more than confused cows. Yet at Málaga—'

'You saw that fight?'

'No, but I listened to the toreros describe it, and those who studied bulls suspected that some spell had been cast.' Suddenly she banged on the table: 'Mr. Shenstone, you clever American who's supposed to know everything, you sat beside him through those fights, six bulls in each—'

'I thought he was praying.'

'He was. The moment he stopped praying his link with the Virgin would be broken.'

'How did you know the Virgin was involved?'

'I didn't.' This so obviously perplexed me that she added: 'But my people watch for me. What I don't see, they see.' Smiling mysteriously, she touched my arm again: 'On that morning the Virgin came down from her pedestal to speak with Don Cayetano—'

'You saw that?'

Ignoring my interruption, she said: 'Do you recall, maybe, an old woman in a shawl who ran out of the church when the Virgin left? Can you guess where she ran to?'

'Your house? Egipciana? What did your spy tell you?'

'She crossed herself three times and said: "Señorita Magdalena, she came down again." And then I knew.'

'You've seen her come down to bestow miracles?'

'She doesn't come to those like me.'

I was about to ask her what other miracles had been performed in that church, but I was interrupted by a loud thumping on her door, and when she opened it I saw Lázaro López standing there. Ignoring me, he caught his sister by the hands, pulled her to him and embraced her vigorously: 'We managed it. Thanks, sister. We managed it.' Then, acknowledging my presence, he asked: 'This one? Does he know?'

'For an americano he's very clever. I did not have to tell him.'

For the first time since I started following the always hectic and often disgraceful career of Lázaro López, he revealed himself as a decent human being, for he said: 'You know bullfighting, Señor Americano. No matador ever had a bull in the Maestranza as fine as that last one. How I wanted to continue the fight, show myself as greater than they had ever seen before. *Saliendo en hombros* through the great gate of Seville. That would almost be worth dying for. To die at the height of my powers, on the horns of a great bull, like Manolete. I'd be remembered forever in bullfight history.' When I saw that he had truly considered allowing the bull to kill him for the glory it would have given him, I felt respect. 'But my sister had warned me: "Lázaro, when the bugle sounds for the sword, you

have half a minute. He dies or you die." So I really had no choice, for I knew that my sister needs me, to protect her.'

If I had ever seen a woman who required no protection from anyone—least of all a brother younger than herself and with no character—it was Magdalena López, the Gypsy fortune-teller, but I thought it best not to say so.

The last I saw of this remarkable pair, she was bending over to tend to his black eye. 'The pigs gave you one, didn't they?' she said almost admiringly, pleased to think that he had again defrauded those who jeered him and had escaped with such a minor wound. Then she saw me about to leave and said: 'Don't try to explain what you saw today. Who would believe you?'

Back in the darkened street I looked to my left at the Church of the Toreros, so splendid and reassuring beside the river, and thought: Virgin, in your fine church you promised Don Cayetano two supreme afternoons, and you bestowed them. Magdalena López, in your snug little house you undertook to keep your brother alive, and you did.

It seemed incredible that a being as noble as the Virgin had engaged in a plaza brawl with a Gypsy fortune-teller from Triana, but in Spain that's the way things sometimes happen.

Their duel was a draw.

ABOUT THE AUTHOR

Universally revered novelist JAMES A. MICHENER was forty before he decided on writing as a career. Prior to that, he had been an outstanding academic, an editor, and a U.S. Navy lieutenant commander in the Pacific theater during World War II. His first book, *Tales of the South Pacific,* won a Pulitzer Prize and became the basis of the award-winning Rodgers and Hammerstein musical *South Pacific.* In the course of the next forty-five years Mr. Michener wrote such monumental best-sellers as *Iberia, Hawaii, The Source, Texas, Alaska,* and *Mexico,* and the memoir *The World is My Home.*

Decorated with America's highest civilian award, the Presidential Medal of Freedom, Mr. Michener has served on the Advisory Council to NASA, holds honorary doctorates in five fields from thirty leading universities, and has received an award from the President's Committee on the Arts and Humanities for his continuing commitment to art in America. He lives in Austin, Texas.

ABOUT THE ILLUSTRATOR

JOHN FULTON is an American *matador de toros* who has lived and practiced his art in Seville for over thirty years.